C000067329

Psychic Empath

Awaken Your Inner Psychic Abilities By
Discovering And Developing Skills Like
Clairvoyance, Telepathy, Healing Mediumship,
Intuition, And Connecting To Your Spirit Guides

Earl Martin

Table of Contents

Chapter One

Instinct and psychic development

I'm not catching what it means to be a Psychic?

A mystic is an individual who professes to utilize extrasensory perception (ESP) to distinguish data that are beyond the intellect, using clairvoyance or special insight, or who performs acts that are evidently baffling by regular laws. Albeit numerous individuals have confidence in mystic capacities, the logical agreement is that there is no verification of the presence of such powers and portrays the training as pseudoscience. "Psychic" is likewise utilized as a descriptive word to depict such capacities.

Mystics include individuals in an assortment of jobs. Some are showy entertainers, for example, organized performers, who utilize different strategies, e.g., prestidigitation, cold perusing, and hot perusing, to create the presence of such capacities for excitement purposes.

Everybody can be Psychic

Mystic mindfulness is the comprehension of human awareness and the maximum capacity of the mind when applied to regular day-to-day existence.

The significance of "mind" originates from Greek, deciphering as "the breath of life." "Psychic," additionally from Greek, signifies "of the spirit, mental."

Psychic mindfulness is a truly conscious understanding of the existence of power or spirit inside us and the intensity of the human personality.

Paranormal or clairvoyant capacities have for quite some time been dreaded and thought of as insidious, hazardous, or essentially superstitious rubbish utilized by cheats to exploit others thought to be uneducated or simply artless.

Clairvoyant and instinctive capacities, similar to the capacity to give profound mending, ought not to be viewed as the endowment of the few – they are the inheritance of everybody on Earth. These capacities are inert inside every one of us – and instinct and mystic advancement can happen through profound practices such as yoga breathing and mantra, and by different types of administration to other people, for example, supplication and otherworldly mending.

Certain methods are explicitly arranged toward building up these capacities, while others are situated toward other objectives. For instance, if you practice yoga breathing strongly over a long period of time, with the end goal of picking up illumination, with no intrigue at all in clairvoyant capacities, you will, in any case, become mystic accordingly.

While everybody can build up their mystic capacities, it may not be a specific person's predetermination to have this as a need. It might be considerably more significant for somebody to get familiar with specific expertise, not legitimately identifying with anything mystic; however, every aptitude can be improved by acquainting a clairvoyant component with it.

All individuals have inert clairvoyant capacities. Mystic instinct is one of the abilities that can most effectively be created. Numerous individuals utilize their instinct regularly and don't much think about how conceivable it is; it is a clairvoyant capacity they are utilizing. The sentiments and feelings that you sense from other individuals are what add to instinct.

However, it is likewise the connected clairvoyant vibrations that make it such an integral asset and experience for some individuals. Creating it very well may be finished with a little focus and assurance and is unquestionably advantageous. It will make you increasingly sure of data you can from instinct and enable you to settle on decisions dependent on it with more noteworthy certainty.

The main all-around perceived advance to building up your mystic instinct is to consistently rehearse reflection and build up your aptitudes here. You can move the abilities you gain from reflection to parts of your life interfacing with other individuals. If you can be loose and open in your communications, you will be progressively prepared to get on the concealed sign and clairvoyant vibrations. Connected to this is rehearsing perception. Here you should concentrate on one specific mental picture and investigate it as much as possible. Building up this expertise implies that you can utilize it intuitively when associating with individuals. It will empower you to detect more completely their entire depth as opposed to simply the self they are exhibiting.

Mystic instinct is obviously connected to other clairvoyant capacities. Pre-perception is an expertise you can take a shot at that will build up your fruitful utilization of instinct. You can rehearse this by centering during specific circumstances, for example, who has gone to the entryway or who is on the opposite finish of a ringing phone. In these circumstances, you ought not to make a decent attempt yet simply unwind and see what faces come into your cognizance. Building this expertise is unmistakably connected to the aptitudes of clairvoyant instinct. The key again is to unwind and give the data a chance to come to you in whatever structure it does. It is critical to unwind and make an effort not to drive an answer. This is the place an advancement of your contemplation abilities will have made a difference.

The majority of the above will truly help with the advancement of your clairvoyant instinct. You can consider creating it further with further developed-centered practice. Another aptitude that will help with this is winding up progressively mindful of your own and other individuals' vitality fields. This is a way that can genuinely upgrade your instinct in a propelled manner. You can utilize your conscious feeling of an individual's vitality and how yours is reacting to it to increase a more profound comprehension of what your instinct is letting you know.

Psychic capacities are neither great nor terrible

Clairvoyant capacities are neither great nor terrible in themselves – it is the manner by which they are utilized that makes them fortunate or unfortunate. If, for instance, you utilize mystic capacity to take a gander at the atmosphere of a patient before giving them otherworldly mending, and you see plainly precisely what part of the quality needs uncommon consideration, and you at that point check out the accurate, attractive vitality required to recuperate that individual, this is clearly something worth being thankful for to do. Assuming, be that as it may, you utilize clairvoyant capacity to fulfill eagerness or carry mischief to another person, this is clearly an abuse. It is as straightforward as that.

The clairvoyant world exists surrounding us. We can't see it or contact it, yet we know it's there. There have been dreadfully numerous encounters to discount as an unimportant incident. Possibly you yourself have had encounters with the mystic world, and that is the reason you are here. Regardless of whether you realize you have mystic capacities, you know somebody who does, or you are simply addressing whether you can manufacture clairvoyant gifts, there's a great deal you have to think about clairvoyant forces and improvement.

Most importantly, understand that everybody has some degree of clairvoyant capacity. It is totally inactive in many people because, as a general public, we've been instructed not to have confidence in things we can't see. Subduing or clarifying ceaselessly your mystic encounters is a certain method to smother your clairvoyant improvement. A few people have a progressively characteristic capacity to take advantage of the mystic world, and whether that is because of nature or sustain, we'll likely never truly know. In any case, if you have an enthusiasm for investigating your clairvoyant nature and an ability to accept, at that point, you are an astounding contender for creating mystic forces.

Everything begins with attention to yourself and your general surroundings. The mystic world is so near us. Unfortunately, we can't feel its quality all the more regularly. The manner in which we can turn out to be progressively mindful of it is through ordinary sessions of unwinding or reflection. Closer your eyes and look at yourself cautiously. Loosen up each muscle, and attempt to concentrate on nothingness. At the point when an idea flies into your head, tenderly drive it out - some find that rehashing a short mantra, again and again, encourages them to keep their mind clear.

This can be a genuine test for certain individuals to simply rehearse the specialty of sitting still and existing without effectively doing anything. It will more than likely take a few practice sessions before you're ready to do it. Be that as it may, when you're ready to calm your brain, you can watch yourself unreservedly. Knowing yourself all around is the way to taking advantage of your mystic forces.

If you've had a mystic encounter previously, ruminate on it and inspect what occurred and how it affected you. If not, at that point, you'll see that after times of normal reflection, you'll turn out to be more on top of yourself and start seeing bunches of little encounters that you can just credit to clairvoyant capacity. At that point, you will be well on your approach to building up your clairvoyant forces.

Mystic improvement and illumination

It is beyond the realm of imagination to expect to pick up edification, as characterized in The Nine Freedoms, without first creating clairvoyant capacities.

At the point when clairvoyant capacities have been created – they ought to be dismissed, except for those required in administration. This will achieve genuine illumination, which is the yogi's objective. The clairvoyant stage can't be passed up as a great opportunity.

Clairvoyant Abilities and How to Awaken Them

Clairvoyant forces can be grown normally. Everybody has intuition, and keeping in mind that some have it more emphatically than others, we as a whole can be conscious of that sense through training. Contemplation obviously is an incredible spot to begin. It's been said on numerous occasions that contemplation is useful for the psyche, body, soul, and by and large prosperity. Putting in a couple of calm minutes without anyone else's input every day truly can help. Work on breathing systems too. Breathe gradually in a manner that feels great to you. Add incense and candles to the experience also.

Keeping a diary is another smart thought for those keen on expanding their clairvoyant capacities. Record all that you experience during reflection. Record the majority of your sentiments. Each picture or felt that goes through your brain may, in the long run, synchronize with the world, so give nearer consideration to what your psyche is letting you know. The capacity to obviously envision occasions, individuals and places in your inner being is an unquestionable requirement if you need increasingly clairvoyant forces. Return and rehash your words frequently. In time, you should begin seeing the things you compose connecting with genuine occasions.

Figure out how to give more consideration to your surroundings consistently. You can use your intuition similarly as you can all your different faculties by utilizing it. Give better consideration to the individuals that encompass you consistently; attempt taking a gander at them and "through" them. Check them out. Notice the earth encompassing everybody and what everyone looks like inside nature. The more attentive you are, the simpler perception will come to you.

If you need to figure out how to be a clairvoyant medium and how to converse with spirits, that will take some time and practice. If you can improve your sixth sense, ponder, and monitor your emotions and pictures in a diary, your clairvoyant capacities will grow normally. Once in a while, we as a whole get pictures and contemplations as signs from our soul guides, heavenly aides, passed on friends and family, or whatnot, and the more you build up your clairvoyant capacities, the better you'll be at selecting those signs that have uncommon implications.

Arousing Psychic Ability and Mystical Experiences

The expression "mystic" has been taken so out of sight setting and has turned out to be so imperfect; it is about difficult to accept we will ever have an otherworldly "homecoming" when seeking the English language for the importance of this term. A clairvoyant is one who uses natural endowments of the Spirit to get and give messages from God to favor others. This might be done in an adjusted state at an elevated level of otherworldly vibration. In any case, a spiritualist or prophet is generally additionally invested with a simply instinctive blessing that is encouraged in a progressively "typical" condition of being. In any case, the mystic gets data on a powerful otherworldly level.

There are numerous assortments of clairvoyant or profound endowments accessible to us. A profoundly open individual may secure and use any number of these endowments. Jesus utilized every one of them in His service. You may, as of now, have them and not understand it. Since the blessings are seen beside or an elevated utilization of the five known faculties, locate, sound, taste, contact, or smell, they are here and there alluded to as the intuition or extrasensory perception (ESP). At the point when an individual starts to stir to their actual self and heavenly potential, otherworldly or mystic blessings will start to rise and create. Having some perspective on these endowments will aid the edification procedure. With such shame and dread associated with the paranormal nowadays, I feel it is critical to disperse any dread you may have of such marvel. Dread of a profound blessing will absolutely be a hindrance to your utilizing it. To be prepared to do similar works that Jesus did, we have to use these magnificent apparatuses. Daddy wouldn't fret in the event that you utilize His apparatuses, so how about we investigate a portion of these endowments.

Hyper vision

Clair signifies "clear." Clairvoyance, or clear vision, enables you to see with your inner consciousness. This blessing enables you to get on data about an individual by observing pictures or images that relate to something going on in someone else's life. An extrasensory individual may see with their physical or profound eyes, holy messengers, spirits, and different pictures in the otherworldly world. This blessing shows at whatever point, the third eye (or sixth chakra) is open and clear and may show in dreams or dreams. God gives us internal vision today, similarly as He did with the prophets of old.

Clairaudience

Another psychic blessing is the endowment of clairaudience, in which messages are gotten from etheric domains through hearing. Individuals having this blessing may hear soul messages perceptibly or inside their brains. This is the blessing Joan of Arc utilized.

Clairsentience

A few people are honored with the endowment of psychometry, or clairsentience, which is the capacity to contact an item and get precise data about the proprietor, in the case of living or passed on. This blessing brings the premonition or "knowing" of something about someone else without having human information of it in advance.

Clairempathy

Clairempathy enables an individual to feel (inside their body or feelings) the emotions, torment, or needs of someone else. At whatever point there is a world disaster or an occurrence where somebody close by is enduring, individuals with this blessing may start to get on this vitality and become a surrogate. If you discover you have unexplained agony or feelings that surface without cause, you might get on someone else's vitality. It is significant for the individual with this blessing to realize how to define profound limits or else clear the vitality from their field.

Clairgustance

Clairgustance has to do with getting a message from the otherworldly domain through the feeling of taste. You might have the option to taste something that you have not eaten or even been close. Ask yourself questions about why you are "tasting" this message. Gracious, taste and see that the Lord is great!

Clairscent

Clairscent enables an individual to smell a scent or smell from another domain. It is likened to the endowment of clear taste or clairgustance. I have smelled roses and other grand fragrances while supplicating. The kingdom of Heaven is close to you, even in your nose!

The Gift of Healing the Sick

As you climb in your otherworldly progress, you may see that you can mend others. My better half's dad was sick from a mishap and slipped into a state of unconsciousness. Specialists at the medical clinic in Burbank, California, demonstrated he had "lost mind mass" and would not be the equivalent regarding subjective capacities. He would truly be told, they stated, be increasingly much the same as "a vegetable" if he lived. They accepted his demise was fast approaching. I quickly contemplated a Bible sacred text, Ecclesiastes 2:12-14, "I saw that shrewdness is superior to indiscretion, similarly as light is superior to anything obscurity." Light is in the Universe and individualized in your very own soul. I approached the "Light" of the mending blessed messenger Raphael to encompass and secure Mr. Morris. I saw these inconceivable circles of light in my inner consciousness. I "felt" he was immaculate, similarly as God made him. The Light entered my very being, and I "knew" he was mended. That is all. I spoke to the Doctor who made all specialists. Our bodies are supernatural gems. They are always being destroyed back to the first and ideal outline of their profound DNA. I accept that the best specialist on earth can play out mending follow-up on the body, yet it is eventually the Highest Doctor of the Universe who sends the vitality to cause the real recuperating.

The specialists at the emergency clinic called our home very energized, searching for my significant other, Cynthia, saying they had seen "a supernatural occurrence." Push your psyche to the edge and consider some fresh possibilities. Those imperceptible photons of light which travel at 186,000 miles for each second gone into that medical clinic room, contacted my father-in-law's body, and in that light, the dying man was resuscitated.

The Skeptics

What human instinct doesn't comprehend, it tries to oppose or devastate. Why should we judge the new, new messages originating from the core of God to His youngsters who have receptive outlooks and are happy to hear that voice today? What might we do with an advanced Noah who purportedly "heard" the voice of God? What might we do with a Moses who separated seas with a walking stick?

Any blessing or activity that brings wellbeing, love, recuperating, adequacy of brain, happiness, harmony, tenderness, goodness, confidence, genuineness, or some other righteousness is of God regardless of what marks the "practitioner" may wear or what profound camp they spend time with.

Your profile vitality is constantly present in your physical body, just like your soul. It is your "attraction" or body power that empowers the correspondence between the mind and different pieces of the body. Psychic vitality associates you with your very own body, other individuals, and their spirits, just as to the Universe or God. At the point when your profound vitality is exhausted, it adversely impacts your physical body and its quality, making it progressively vulnerable to malady and different diseases. If your body needs supplements for ordinary working, think the amount more your soul needs the supporting of the petition, reflection, contemplation, and custom to keep it alive!

Enchanted Experiences

The otherworldly experience that has been deductively recorded for quite a long time is as yet drilled by people today. We have numerous names for these profoundly changing encounters. It is up to the person regarding how to react to them. We might be kept to the confinement of the physical body, yet our forces of the brain are most certainly not. The frame of mind, confidence, and conviction have a significant effect on the way we react to a circumstance. An individual might be imprisoned for wrongdoing. The individual in question has a decision of reaction. They can enable their heart to solidify, or they may utilize their brain and time for composing a smash hit! When you are driven by your heart and not your condition, the sky is the limit. I urge you to acknowledge the mysterious encounters that come to you. They are to instruct, illuminate, and stir you.

The distinction between instinct and psychic advancement

Like such a significant number of words, "instinct" is utilized contrastingly by various individuals. One method for taking a gander at the instinct is as the "voice" of the Divine Spirit inside showing through the brain – the most noteworthy piece of ourselves "talking" to us. Accordingly, instinct is naturally otherworldly in nature – while psychic forces are not really profound by any stretch of the imagination.

Seen in this light, instinct is the most significant staff we have because it is through instinct that we perceive heavenly truth. It is instinct overall that will disclose to you whether the substance of this site is valid. The troublesome part is "hearing" the instinct, in the midst of the racket of common uproar we fill our brains with consistently. Furthermore, when heard, the instinct must be perceived the truth about. Very regularly, individuals botch what they need to be valid for the voice of instinct, revealing to them that it is valid.

The most effective method to build up the instinct

The more we tune in to our instinct – and the more we follow up on what we hear – the better our instinct will get. The more honest we are, and the more we commit ourselves to truth, the more we will pull in truth and have the option to remember it.

Immaculateness of the thought process is additionally crucial for creating instinct. If we truly need the eternal truth, with the goal that we can utilize this information to help other people, and if we put enough energy into discovering it, we will discover it and remember it. This is ensured by the Divine law.

Administration and profound practices, as referenced above, are additionally great approaches to build up the instinct.

There are numerous varieties of psychics out there, and it may be the case that you are just barely starting to find your psychic blessings and abilities or that you are a prepared and experienced psychic.

A portion of the psychic capacities you may have could incorporate clairvoyance, mediumship, supernatural power, precognition, levitation, and diverting. Being psychic relies upon the kinds of psychic capacity you have, or it might be that you are talented enough to have more than one sort of capacity.

If you are an extrasensory psychic, at that point, you can utilize your psychic capacities to respond to questions and comprehend circumstances to which you would not have the option to generally discover answers or see completely. Online readings psychic experts offer might be as clairvoyance, or you could telephone a psychic to discover the solution to your inquiries by means of this station.

A few psychics are gifted in mediumship, which is the capacity to speak with the soul world: individuals who have passed away however who still hold a connection with the living. If you have physic capacities of this nature, at that point, you can possibly have the option to channel messages from the soul world to the living. Proficient mediums regularly go about as transmitters of messages from the soul world to the perished individual's relatives or friends and family.

Supernatural power is otherwise called psychokinesis and is the capacity to move items utilizing the intensity of the mind alone. If you have supernatural abilities, they may need sharpening so as to have the option to consummate them. If your psychic capacities exhibit themselves as precognition, at that point, it implies you can anticipate occasions before they occur, once in a while in dreams, at different occasions in waking dreams. Being a psychic with levitation abilities is uncommon and implies you can drift over the ground.

There are obviously many further kinds of psychic capacity. Being psychic is to have some part of psychic capacity; it may be that you haven't understood your psychic capacities yet, and they stay lethargic. There are strategies and procedures you can use to carry your psychic capacities to the fore. A smart thought may be to visit with psychic individuals such as yourself to discover progressively what your abilities mean.

The accompanying psychic forces are frequently alluded to as the 4 clairs. If you are confounded about what sort of psychic capacity you have, these 4 psychic forces may assist you with an explanation.

1. Hyper vision is the capacity to see individuals that have been disregarded. It

likewise enables you to see dreams and pictures that are not of this world.

2. Clairaudio is the point at which you hear a voice either inside or outside your head when you are separated from everyone else. You likewise can hear messages in tunes and other individuals' discussions.

3. Clairsentience enables you to get messages through your sentiments or feelings. Have you at any point had a premonition about a significant choice you are going to make dependent on research and rationale? Just to discover, ultimately, you have a compelling impulse to alter your perspective.

4. Claircognizance is the point at which you simply know things. Messages are coordinated through the chakra at the highest point of your head through your mind. Individuals with this ability can see future occasions and simply appear to realize what will occur. Individuals with this blessing don't generally comprehend why they appear to know to such an extent.

Psychic Ability and Spirituality

Psychic capacity is just the capacity to speak with weaves of vitality that are over the 'typical' level of physical reality. Perusing future occasions, past occasions, otherworldly learning, and directing the 'dead' are indications of associating with explicit weaves of vitality. The term 'psychic' has turned into an umbrella term to include numerous aptitudes and capacities that are viewed as paranormal or supernatural. Developing these aptitudes can truly be classed under 'correspondence.'

It makes the theme of otherworldliness far more clear when we comprehend that 'otherworldliness' is extremely a correspondence with soul. It generally has been and presumably consistently will. The different meanings of 'soul' change from religion to religion and conviction to conviction, yet the pith is the equivalent. It is about correspondence with the soul. The most precise correspondence is continually going to be immediate correspondence. It is the equivalent of any verbal correspondence with someone else. Being there and doing genuine talking is continually going to be more exact than recycled data. This is the place psychic capacity comes in.

Psychic capacity is just an extension of our arrangement of specialized apparatuses. Where there may have been no channel with which to tune in and address soul or other enthusiastic substances, psychic capacities help to open up these ways. Having said this, psychic capacity all by itself doesn't approach profound correspondence. Profound correspondence, like any correspondence, requires an expectation to associate - for this situation to the soul. The language and resources of the association are then utilized and created to pick up familiarity and comprehension.

A giving up of the sense of self's wants is essential when figuring out how to impart psychically to the soul. This procedure is upheld by aides and substances that hold the way open at explicit planes and measurements. For instance, while some might be at any rate ready to comprehend the limitless soul, most will experience issues with moving completely into boundless awareness. This is simply because the living example of the brain is excessively solid. The more established or progressively experienced we are, the more solidified these examples become. Getting around this requires committed practice, nuance, and a consistent will to refine and comprehend self-dominance.

The cutting-edge world has a propensity for making individuals dependent on semantics, and this also is something that we should relinquish. Semantics and words become futile in the long run, just the genuine implying that words and ideas point to hold genuine strengthening and comprehension. This is the place psychic capacity gives an amazing chance. Psychic capacity enables us to see profoundly amazing and ideas to the source. In shapes, fragrances, sounds, and structures, these weaves of vitality grow and develop, driving us through their ways and expelling us through our own. The channel that is framed winds up more grounded and clearer than the natural body we live in would ever be. This turns into our course to the soul, our association, and our correspondence. It is here that we come to see the soul with our very own eyes, hear the soul with our very own ears and feel soul with our very own heart.

Tips about Psychic Abilities

A psychic is an individual who has the ability to perceive and recognize data that isn't seen or felt by individuals who are non-psychic. This limit referred to extensively as Extrasensory Perception or ESP, is the essential contrast between a psychic and some other individuals. Psychics work in various manners. We have the individuals who understood airs, who can survey by contact, who can understand minds, and the individuals who can impart adequately with individuals who are longer with us, to give some examples. As indicated by most psychics, all people have an essential psychic capacity or what is named a hunch. This instinctual mindfulness is the base of most psychic capacities, and by and large, it is a dormant capacity that is sharpened by long stretches of involvement and advancement of expertise.

While the facts confirm that most psychics are brought into the world with a characteristic ability, today, numerous individuals accept that it is conceivable to form into being a psychic. As almost all human beings are blessed with considerable potential for psychic ability, it is very possible to build up that ability. Finding out about the different books that are accessible will help massively in understanding the different subtleties there are to the specialty of being psychic. Stepping through an examination that checks the psychic capacity that an individual has will help in distinguishing the scope of the capacity to see things other than the self-evident.

When an individual's psychic capacity is determined, at that point, there are numerous approaches to build up those capacities and become an undeniable psychic. The most significant aspect of psychical capacity is the requirement for focus and contemplation. To completely sharpen any or every single psychical capacity, it is significant that an individual gains proficiency with these two fundamental things. Psychics are individuals who are presented with numerous things which are not seen by those of us who are non-psychic. They have to develop their capacity to withstand the assault of the most outrageous of feelings and sentiments and ought to likewise have the option to see with their inner consciousness without getting by and by including. For this, it is significant that they figure out how to think completely.

Another method for creating psychical capacities is to keep up an uplifting viewpoint towards life. Numerous specialists have repeated the significance of this energy by talking about its capacity to open the psyche to the numerous potential outcomes that can exist. Being loose is essential to a psychic. Any demonstration of pressure will hamper the psychical capacity and not take into consideration a total or genuine vision/understanding. Loosening up the brain and the body will help in the opening of the "third eye," the most significant workforce to be a psychic, and will prompt advancement in turning into a psychic.

Psychic mindfulness has an extremely different exhibit of examples through which it tends to be communicated. Everybody is extraordinary, and as a result of this, individuals will, in general, see the universe of their existential encounters through varying courses of action of vitality detecting and impact. As such, there are various manners by which psychic capacities can show. This is due to the fact that the base vitality of being is exceptionally flexible and synergistic.

People work through a progression of criticism circles on a physiological level. Huge numbers of these input circles are real examples of protection from genuine nature. In order to stir and adjust to the genuine wellspring of psychic capacities that dwells at the core of being, one must figure out how to discharge these rehashing examples of obstruction. This, therefore, opens up the vitality designs inside and clears blockages that would one way or another restrict the maximum capacity of articulation.

At last, this is arousing to a more prominent articulation of the totality of awareness. This really goes past the fanciful degree of presence and even the utilization of psychic recognition at this level. This shouldn't imply that those psychic capacities and impressions of other-dimensional degrees of vitality have no reason. What it means is that these capacities are all the more effectively used when they are acknowledged and realized inside an example of stirred and edified conduct. This implies the disintegration of egoic examples of obstruction and negligible passionate connections that alone serve to invalidate the unrestricted idea of unity.

A remote survey is generally thought of with regards to knowledge and data gathering. This is because numerous remote review strategies were in reality created by military knowledge projects, for example, the C.I.A. The truth of this is these methods are basically an exacting convention for using psychic mindfulness in an extremely straightforward manner that is intended for the exactness of data procured for explicit targets. The get-together of precise data for explicit targets is the essential goal of the conventional remote review.

Remote survey strategies and preparation, for the most part, don't concern the advancement and improvement of the watcher's conscious mindfulness. It performed in an extremely inflexible condition under foreordained conditions. It is workable for anybody to use their higher faculties along these lines, yet except if accentuation is set on getting to be stirred through the arrival of a sense of self, there will next to no genuine advancement in a general capacity.

Remote survey procedures are, for the most part, restricted because of the reality they are performed from the wrong point of view of a different I, me, and mine. It is viewed as a person's capacity to get to a surge of data that is promptly accessible. Remote review is viewed as a path for an individual to connect and get data that is "past themselves."

As one advances to higher conditions of conscious mindfulness, it turns out to be clear this is a wrong point of view. Everything and everybody exists as a unified entire inside various elements of full vitality. These measurements increment in their nuance and interconnectedness as they arrive at the eye or core of internal stillness that dwells at the focal point of all of the room time. Everything is an outflow of this quiet vacancy of endless potential, and from this, EVERYTHING is communicated.

This is how the mechanics of remote survey is conceivable. At the core of everything dwells the example of everything else. Remote review strategies basically direct somebody to arouse to this inside themselves. The best psychic preparation enables the individual to get into the framework of this endless articulation and reappear, changed and stirred to the more prominent truth of their reality.

Chapter Two

Indications of psychic abilities

Numerous individuals accept they may have psychic capacities and wish to examine the probability with another person. Be that as it may, if these emotions are communicated to a doubter, it's simple for them to be rejected as "only an incident." Choose somebody receptive with whom you can share the indications of psychic capacities that you have encountered.

There is no science yet that can completely disclose to you whether you are psychic or not. There are a few tests that can affirm you have a tendency for psychic capacities, yet the outcomes can't be outright. Eventually, you may simply need to start to confide in yourself and your very own involvement without affirmation from an outside source.

Numerous psychics propose that contemplation is a manner by which they tap into their psychic capacities and reinforce them. Along these lines, with the goal for you to show signs of individual improvement understanding and the mental image of your own psychic capacities, it might be a smart thought to rehearse contemplation. This can further explain and build up any aptitudes you may have.

The specialty of reflection is an ability that can be scholarly, and it requires control and propensity. However, the advantages are monstrous. Following are a few rules to help as you start a reflective practice.

Arrangement for reflection:

1. Protection: Find a peaceful zone somewhere, and wipe out the probability of being hindered by the TV, radio, phone, or someone else.
2. Get Comfortable: Find an agreeable seat, get into a place that you can unwind in, and ensure you are neither very hot nor very cold.
3. Unwind: Rest your head, close your eyes, and inhale profound, slow breaths. Know about grasping your jaw or pressure in your shoulders and deliberately enable your entire body to simply give up.

The reflection procedure:

1. Breathing: Focus your whole personality on your relaxation. Tune in to how it sounds in your mind; you can hear your breaths being attracted and hear them being discharged once more. Take in on a check of four and out on a tally of four.
2. Aim: Ask that you be made mindful of any psychic aptitudes you may have and believe that you will be given an answer.
3. Remain Focused: Whenever you feel your mind begin to meander and you become mindful of the outside world, bring it back onto your breathing again and center it there.

Observe which side effects of psychic capacities emerge as you contemplate. When you are completely loose and responsive, you may begin to detect and feel what a few psychics call "psychic vibrations." You may end up mindful of a "knowing" sensation, you may see pictures or hues, and you may hear words.

These can be depicted as side effects of psychic capacities. With standard practice, the time required to arrive at the purpose of center in contemplation will be decreased, and your psychic sensations will keep on developing.

Do you ever think about whether you have psychic capacities? Do you will, in general, disregard a sensation that this has happened before encounters, or think about examples of your spot-on instinct as just happenstances? Do you overlook the bizarre things you experience or investigate? A vast dominant part of us have upgraded psychic capacities in some shape or structure, and it is normally a grown-up watchman or parent that first notification indications of our psychic conduct.

Here and there, psychic individuals are thought of as abhorrent or into dark enchantment. This is just false. We as a whole have a type of psychic conduct; however, a large number of us don't have a clue how to perceive the manifestations, overlook them, or simply haven't found them yet. It won't be long until psychic capacities begin to appear.

Look at these psychic side effects and signs that may demonstrate you have psychic capacities. Perhaps you will arrive at a resolution and acknowledge you are psychic, all things considered. It's a matter of comprehending what to pay special attention to.

1. More significant levels of instinct.

If you have ever realized who is approaching the telephone before getting there, who a book is from before checking the cover, or you had ever anticipated an occasion before it happened, you have a more elevated level of instinct. This is a stage towards finding a psychic blessing inside yourself.

2. You have encountered a sensation that this has happened before on many occasions.

If you always feel like you have been somewhere before despite the fact that you haven't, and if you have an incredible sentiment of commonality with individuals, sports, and things, you might encounter this feels familiar. A sensation that this has happened before is a certain sign that you have a type of psychic capacity.

3. Dreams are typical for you.

If you have had dreams of future occasions: things occurring in the following hour or three days from now, you have psychic capacities. If you have them in your fantasies or inside your day-by-day wakeful life, you may have the psychic blessing.

4. A premonition that is constantly exact.

If you simply "know" something before it occurs, and you can detect the occasions of what's going on or what is going to occur, this is a solid indication of a psychic.

5. Clairvoyant examples.

Do you have an inclination that you can send messages through your psyche? Have you at any point felt like you are perusing another person's manner of thinking? Have you encountered a brain-to-mind association? If you have encountered this once in a while, you have some type of clairvoyance, which is a psychic manifestation.

6. Fabulous scale expectations and hunches.

Have you at any point recorded occasions that you "know" will occur later on? Have they occurred? If you have set aside the effort to record hunches or educate somebody concerning them before they really occur, and after that, they happen, you have a psychic blessing.

7. Psychometry is clear.

Psychometry is known as the psychic capacity that enables a person to detect or encounter the historical backdrop of an individual or item by contacting them or it. Psychics have learning and power since they "know" about individuals, sports, articles, and energies simply by being somewhere or by basically contacting a person or thing. For instance, an individual who has the psychometry psychic capacity can hold a person's hand and sense and experience their past. They may even observe pictures or experience scents, sounds, and tastes starting there in time.

8. Incredible clear dreams.

Individuals with psychic capacities will, in general, have amazingly distinctive dreams and can recall detail for detail after they alert. The images in their fantasies have profound established implications, and they generally offer a type of extraordinary comprehension for the person's beneficial experience. Numerous individuals who have clear dreams likewise have repeating dreams that recount a story and that are demonstrative of what's going on, all things considered.

9. You sense inconvenience.

This is an immediate inclination where you simply know somebody you cherish is in a tough situation. It hits you with extraordinary effect and, in some cases, with an incredible sentiment of extreme dread. There is no clarification for it aside from that you realize something is profoundly amiss with somebody you adore.

10. You tell what's to come.

This is one of the conspicuous characteristics of an individual with psychic capacities. Advising the future to your loved ones, at that point, having it really happen is one of the main ways that demonstrate you are psychic.

11. You can recuperate.

Have you at any point laid your hands on somebody who is enduring or sick? Did you at that point see a positive change in this wiped-out person? Numerous individuals that have psychic capacities can likewise recuperate others with their vitality.

12. Hearing sounds.

Have you at any point heard sounds that others don't? Do you always ask why nobody else is hearing rings, blares, and tolls? These sounds can really be a sign of a not-so-distant future occasion, and they can inform you concerning certain occasions that will happen.

13. You can detect two places without a moment's delay.

This is unquestionably one of the more grounded psychic capacities and signs that you might be psychic. If you have ever been at home or in one spot that is commonplace to you yet sense occasions and encounters that are occurring over the world in various nations, you are undoubtedly psychic. If you have dreams of these occasions while they are going on and really feel just as you have moved to the goal as it is occurring, you have increased psychic capacities.

Being psychic is anything but an alarming issue, and you shouldn't feel frightful of your capacities. Consider these devices and aptitudes as exceptional endowments and attempt to get familiar with every capacity so you can utilize these to their maximum capacity.

Numerous psychics are amazingly significant to individuals who have not yet found their own psychic capacities. Individuals go to psychic people for an assortment of reasons, regardless of whether it is for direction and backing or uncovering riddles and illuminating wrongdoings. Hold onto your psychic endowments as one of nature's most dominant blessings and use them to help other people in a constructive way.

Signs You Might Be Psychic

Sign #1: Two Glasses of Wine Make You More Insightful

Ever know about individuals all of a sudden "seeing" the answer for an issue when they're unwinding and not effectively captivating their psyches? For example, you're scrubbing down, and you have an abrupt knowledge into taking care of an issue at work. A similar sort of data may likewise come to you while you're thinking or doing yoga. Studies have demonstrated that these practices appear to change our mind wave movement — frequently making our frontal projection calm down. Be that as it may, in my experience, these exercises additionally appear to "open" individuals who are psychic much more! Psychic capacities can frequently sit unobtrusively; at that point, they abruptly rise when we're not centered on them.

Presently comes the interesting part: Let's say your most grounded flashes of knowledge show up when you're unwinding with a glass of wine. In particular, if you drink two mixed refreshments inside, state, an hour and a half period, you simply appear to "know" exact data about individuals without their having let you know. That is a solid sign that you might be psychic, which you may expel, accepting that you're only somewhat blasted and overemotional.

Sign #2: Your New Friend Looks Blue — or Red

Psychics see individuals in an unexpected way. This is often due to the fact that they are encountering synesthesia, a condition wherein faculties are swapped. Have you at any point met another individual whom you connected with shading, a bloom, or a scene? Have you at any point heard melodic notes encompassing somebody? These flashes of tangible discernment occur inside, and when they occur, are clear — the vast majority, however, don't discuss them, for dread that doing so would sound excessively unusual.

From the beginning, I encountered synesthesia and regularly observed individuals in hues. In time, I started to comprehend that this diverse method for seeing individuals was not something to be frightened by, yet that it was, truth be told, a supportive device. For instance, I came to get that if an individual seemed "blue" to me, the person was a characteristic healer or instructor, and I would feel entirely great around the individual's vitality. If I considered somebody to be "red," I comprehended this was an individual who was encountering pressure and tension and was regularly irascible — a sign that I should stay away. Around particularly energetic individuals, I would likewise hear sensitive music, similar to a precious stone breeze toll being rung together. This synesthesia still occurs for me today, despite everything I use it. If it's transpiring, grasp it, and notice the data it's passing on to you.

Sign #3: Your Gut Has Saved Your Life (or Your Budget)

Maybe you've had a solid inclination in the past that you expected to go to a store at a specific time... at that point proceeded to locate the precise thing you'd recently been scanning all over for, in your accurate size, in stock, and 50 percent off. Or then again, maybe you've had a compelling impulse while driving, to maintain a strategic distance from a specific path home...only to discover later that there had been a horrible mishap on the course you were on. A large portion of us have had these premonitions — otherwise called natural pulls. However, a psychic draw is significantly progressively clear: It feels practically like having a magnet in your sunlight-based plexus territory that pulls you toward or away from something. This inclination is normally combined with an unmistakable feeling of knowing (which is called claircognizance).

Sign #4: Your Dreams Seep into Your Waking Life in Surprising Ways

Possibly you imagined around evening time that your perished mother addressed you about where your missing wristband was — just to discover it in that definite spot the following morning. Or then again, perhaps you were grinding away and abruptly had a blazing picture, in a "dream," of holding a trophy as though you were winning something — just to discover, minutes after the fact, that you were being granted advancement. Perhaps you even longed for somebody you hadn't found in a very long time, just to keep running into the individual the following day. Despite the fact that you attempt to reject or overlook these encounters, they keep on occurring. It's ordinary, I've found, for individuals to get "scared" about dreams and fantasies that incorporate supposed incidents.

I think firsthand about the significance of not rejecting these psychic encounters when they happen, yet now and again, even I neglect to focus. As of late, I was on a plane, doing chip away at another PC. At the point when my airline steward gave me my beverage, I had an abrupt glimmer: a picture of it spilling onto my PC console. Be that as it may, I was extremely parched, and the flight was smooth, and there was a strong cup holder inserted in my plate. In this way, I chose to be legitimate and reject the picture I had seen. Not 10 minutes after the fact, the man in the seat before me all of a sudden, and powerfully, leaned back his seat right back. It whacked into my PC, spilling club soft drink all over my console. I really wanted to understand that the opposite side had attempted to alarm me by giving me the feeling — and I was helped to remember that it is so imperative to respect those messages.

These events and feelings — these "synchronicities" or "important fortuitous events" — all simply uncover that you are psychically on top of the universe. Furthermore, it is imperative to be aware of them and not to expel them since they regularly help us connect all the more completely with each other; and, at times, can even caution us of a conceivable peril ahead. Being psychic is not something to be terrified of. It implies we are more associated than we could even dream and more put resources into one another's encounters. Regarding your psychic capacities will enable you to feel that association.

Chapter Three

Phases of Psychic Development

Turning into a psychic isn't simple, as you need to figure out how to awaken your capacities and use them in understanding your will. There are additionally various stages on the most proficient method to utilize them without limit, and the learning procedure may take quite a while so as to create.

The following are the three essential phases of psychic improvement:

Stage 1

Tarot cards

Trying things out. Psychic capacities are here and there stirred intentionally by attempting to try things out. To be sure we all are brought into the world with various psychic forces, and the individuals who are keen on getting to be psychics, in any case, if they know about their forces or, do whatever it takes not to play with various items and instruments associated with the said art.

These incorporate Ouija sheets, tarot cards, runes, just as books that acquaint them with the universe of psychic forces. There are likewise schools that train people into getting to be psychics, and they start with learning elusive jargon so as to know the rudiments of the training.

Stage 2

Ouija board

Realizing the presence of your forces. Not those who have played with Ouija sheets and tarot cards or the individuals who have attempted to bring spirits only for the experience really get the opportunity to understand their psychic capacities. Yet, the ones who had the option to move beyond these games at that point become mindful of the real presence of their forces and are presently on the center street to understanding their maximum capacity.

These individuals currently become equipped for "perusing the field" or seeing through an individual's psyche and transferring it back. Psychics who have arrived at this stage are currently fit for controlling a portion of their endowments; however, not yet without limit. A number of working psychics are right now at this stage, as they can peruse their customers' brains.

Stage 3

Psychic

Getting a handle on the "higher vitality." Most of the present dependable psychics are found in Stage 3. They have a bigger number of abilities than those in Stage 2, and simultaneously they are equipped for controlling their forces in agreement with their own desires.

These psychics have just achieved divination and are never again subject to articles and instruments so as to make their forecasts. They can see through their customers' brains and not just reveal to them what they are thinking; they likewise get the opportunity to give solid counsel on what their customers ought to do about the issue they saw.

Since they are increasingly fit in taking care of their forces, these individuals at that point become qualified of getting to be psychic advocates, instructors, and aides, particularly to people who are new to the art and need to find out about utilizing their very own psychic endowments.

The accompanying stages will demonstrate to you that you are so near 'flicking on the light switch' and awakening from Gergef's 'dozing man.' The stages don't really occur in a specific request, they are not unchangeable, and you may encounter a few at once. The accompanying request does anyway mirror the request for the experience of numerous on the voyage, and there seems to be an efficient way to deal with the improvement procedure. A few people will experience every one of them, others a couple. Generally speaking; nonetheless, you will create at a pace that is actually directly for you.

Huge numbers of the stages are related to the melding of the passionate, vitality body and the profound body, which is a crucial fundamental piece of the improvement procedure.

1. Life Crisis

This stage doesn't really need to happen to everybody on the psychic way on the off chance that they pay heed to the rocks at a beginning period. In any case, the move towards wishing to create on a psychic level is frequently gone before by a real existence dramatization. This can be anything from a befuddled youth to an ongoing separation.

2. Increased Awareness

This is the point at which you begin to see things out of the edge of your eye. This can likewise begin with seeing 'masses' of shading or twirling energies. For other people, it will be the start of hearing messages in your psyche, clear dreams, hunches, and thinking you are either going distraught, or the brain is playing stunts. Individuals regularly overlook the stones here and expel what their increased faculties are attempting to let them know.

3. Extreme touchiness

Becoming increasingly touchy to analysis and other individuals' perspectives. At this stage, you start to realize that you can feel other individuals' sentiments, disarray, and a feeling of, 'am I typical' wins at this stage.

4. Looking

The quest for material that clarifies the weird encounters starts. This is regularly done discreetly through dread of mocking. Additionally, a powerful urge to discover 'similar' people start. It is at this stage you start to truly scrutinize your mental soundness! This is the final turning point. From this phase forward, you will go through your time on earth, scanning for answers to life's inquiries. There might be rests in the middle of yet you will consistently be interested. It winds up like a tingle you can't scratch.

5. Beginning to go to bat for yourself

Be careful! The compliant will all of a sudden start supporting themselves and won't take any hogwash. This might be the present moment as it is just the beginning. A solid establishment has not yet been developed; however, the wheels will have been gotten underway.

6. Feeling alone/misjudged

At this stage, the creating psychic has normally discovered material to in part clarify their advantage and individuals of a similar sort. Sadly at this stage, those frequently nearest to the individual will need to crush their accomplice's/companion's new intrigue since they feel (however won't let it be known) undermined by the new 'leisure activity.' The psychic will regularly be approached by a 'concerned' relative about how they are getting into a mysterious or being mentally programmed and how it is all jibber-jabber. If you don't have this stage, you are fortunate!!

This prompts a very befuddled psychic. Is it wrong to proceed? What would it be a good idea for me to do? Am I frantic? Typically the choice is to continue unobtrusively and not impart the freshly discovered information to your quick companions.

7. I can't do it

Sentiments of frailty surface very well at this stage. The creating psychic see others moving at a quicker speed. They can't work out how to speed their own advancement however become progressively discouraged due to the speed their psychic friends are moving at around them. For some, the inverse may occur; this will be they believe they are moving too immediately, terrified by the experience and needing to back it off or shut it off due to the fact that the duty feels overpowering.

Envision awakening into a weird and obscure world to you. If you are one of the fortunate rare sorts of people who might be very inquisitive and would appreciate awakening in the new, the new would seem an overwhelming spot until you had become acclimated to it. For some, they start to wake up in this new world; they attempt to deny themselves the reality they are awakening somewhere diverse in the expectation things can remain the equivalent, the commonplace and understood, 'safe place.' This will proceed until the creating psychic is never again frightened and wishes to grasp the 'new world' they are awakening to – this can take a little while.

We have all sooner or later in our life dreaded change. The stunt in beating progress dread is to pause for a minute to quickly advance life to how it will be if we continue as before. Life can't change except if we change; only trusting it will change prompts dissatisfaction. In your psyche, quick forward your life to how it will be once change has occurred. You will before long observe change is an energizing choice!

8. Needing quietness/to be separated from everyone else

The faculties are as yet honing, as they are doing so, it is likely at this stage the creating psychic turns out to be touchy to boisterous commotions; they may discover they can't stand the radio playing or the sound of raised voices. Regularly they will need to be in an open space or feel a solid should be in the wide-open, an expanded wish to spend periods alone mulling over or 'gazing out the kitchen window.' Your body is revealing to you it wishes to reflect. During this stage, it is important to locate a normal calm spot during the day to maintain a strategic distance from fractiousness.

9. Acknowledgment that your activity/conditions are not directly for you

This is the start of figuring out how to see the blocks!! Frequently individuals will hold up until they are made excess or sacked (the rock) before they can see they have outgrown their activity/conditions/relationship or that their work environment or home doesn't coordinate with their newly discovered mindfulness. This is frequently a terrible stage since it is tied in with an understanding that your life has regularly been a trade-off (not generally) up until this point. The troublesome piece is the boldness to give up and proceed onward.

Traveling through this stage frequently turns into a hindrance for a great many people and postpones their improvement. This stage is tied in with splitting ceaselessly from the choices 'made for you' throughout everyday life and 'what you have done to satisfy another'. It is tied in with breaking free of the profession you picked because it satisfied your folks, the relationship you remained in for comfort, or the activity you do, for the cash.

Likely the most significant factor in picking the psychic way and building up your expertise, as well as could be expected, is about validness. You can't be a genuinely credible psychic except if you are straightforward with yourself. The individuals who are not genuine with themselves frequently dread the psychic way. The individuals who are straightforward with themselves grasp it!

10. Feeling surrendered

This part doesn't really happen to everybody in a psychic way.

At this stage, loved ones begin to leave your life, or they have all the earmarks of being left. The creating psychic never again feel associated with those they have been partners with for quite a long time. Amazing structures start to deteriorate. All that you thought to be genuine/are joined to self-destruct.

How discouraging!! This is really an awesome stage, giving you ensure you stretch your view past the present circumstance. How would you fix a forsaken structure? Well, you don't! First, you need to wreck it with the goal that you assemble another, more grounded one in its place.

This stage is tied in with seeing through any dreams. Through this stage, we find what is genuine. We truly reveal to ourselves lies! We let ourselves know all is well when it's definitely not. We disclose to ourselves it's terrible when obviously it's alright. At the point when all is detracted from us, we start to comprehend the excellence of the Universe. We build up an extraordinary comprehension of what is extremely significant and figure out how to profoundly welcome the little things throughout everyday life. Incidental data progresses toward becoming random data once this stage is finished. What appeared to be pulverizing doesn't convey a similar feeling it did beforehand.

Wild weeping for no obvious explanation is a piece of this stage. This is because the cells of the body are beginning to lose old memory, clearing a path for the solid capacity to see into your very own and other individuals' lives.

11. Expanded capacity

The psychic faculties, as a rule at this point, are creating with an awesome and firm establishment. The capacity to 'read' individuals is frequently actually very solid by this stage.

12. Detox

This phase for certain individuals comes at an early stage; for other people, it comes significantly later. If you are overlooking it, a physical ailment will regularly need to surface to demonstrate to you (a rock). The time allotment you have been overlooking the need for this, the heavier the physical ailment.

At this stage, the time has come to tidy up your body, and if it has not occurred as of now, your considerations. As the capacity to channel higher energies than your own expands, it is imperative the channel the energies are utilizing is a 'spotless' one. If it isn't, as happens with a lot of psychics, not extremely decent physical disease starts to happen. If you decline to detox, the impact is somewhat similar to stuffing a potato up a fumes pipe.

Detoxing means fasting for a couple of days. There are various fasts you can do, from just drinking water for a day or somewhere in the vicinity to having darker rice for breakfast, lunch, and supper for as long as ten days. You should do a colon purge; eat a lot of new leafy foods. Eat less sugar and meat. Limit your caffeine admission. Avoid low vitality nourishment, for example, takeaways and microwave suppers. If you smoke, drink a lot of liquor, or are dependent on any type of medications (legitimate or illicit), at that point, either stop or get help to stop.

If it's not too much trouble note, ingesting unlawful medications is a low vitality practice, accordingly impeding to yourself as well as any individual you might peruse for. Because of the reality, it is a low vitality act, you will draw in a low vitality soul, and you won't have the option to continue your vitality at a sufficiently high vibration to channel effectively. It would be an over-the-top hop from being low vitality to directing high vitality. Long haul, individuals who do this will cut off the lights will blow!

Chapter Four

Activities for Psychic Abilities

Building up your psychic capacities is a procedure. It requires some investment to fabricate certainty and trust in your capacity. Working with apparatuses like the Tarot or pendulums is one approach to get to your internal knowing, yet like some other learning, it takes practice to create quality. So here, you'll locate some astounding activities to enable you to adjust in and tune.

A portion of these activities originate from the holy messengers through Sally, our holy messenger advisor, and some from my very own aides who offered motivation as I arranged material for different workshops, others originate from our companions and guests… all are offered with adoration, and the longing to enable you…

The greater part of these activities has been tried on numerous occasions throughout the years by my understudies, so they are demonstrated to be viable. Figure out how to examine the vitality around you, work with your fringe vision, play with a remote review, venture yourself forward into the following day, escape your body… the more you get your psychic self associated with your life, the more you will see, feel, hear and know with your internal faculties.

Fun Activities for Psychic Development

Psychic capacities resemble every single other sort of capacity – the more you learn and practice, the more talented you become. You may believe it's precarious to rehearse psychic abilities, yet very are various fun ways you can test yourself, regardless of whether alone or with companions. Just as being pleasant, these activities and games fill a helpful need in building up your psychic muscle in a manner of speaking. Why not track how you jump on with the goal that you can follow your improvement?

1. Foreseeing the Future

Despite the fact that forecast is a disputable theme in the psychic world, and a great many people accept that the future can't be completely anticipated because of unrestrained choice, trying different things with expectations is a valuable method to sharpen your precognition aptitudes. Attempt to:

- predict the result of a game coordinate
- state who is on the telephone before you answer it
- predict a significant news story that will happen in the coming 10 days
- keep a fantasy journal and note down any prescient/precognitive dreams

2. Clairvoyance Practice

Clairvoyance is effectively polished if you have a willing individual to rehearse on – essentially send or transmit a color, or a word, or a shape, and check whether your beneficiary can get on it; at that point, swap, and check whether you can get on their considerations.

Zener cards are likewise a well-known method for testing clairvoyance; on the off chance that you don't have a sly accomplice on your psychic experience, you can rehearse with these without anyone else's input. Simply have the heap of cards faces down before you and experience them individually, taking note of your forecasts, and after that, check.

You can likewise rehearse clairvoyance on unconscious beneficiaries, for example, by willing an alien to pivot and take a gander at you. That is innocuous enough and can be compelling, yet be mindful so as not to exceed moral limits on the off chance that you are attempting to influence somebody who has not given their assent.

3. Psychometry Vibrations

Psychometry is the craft of detecting psychic vibrations from perusing a physical item. This is most effortless to do in a gathering – have everybody bring along a little close-to-home article, at that point, blend them up and pick one to peruse from. This has the favorable position that you'll get moment affirmation of how near the imprint you are.

Nonetheless, you can likewise rehearse an assortment of psychometry all alone. Utilize a photograph (from a magazine, site, or paper) of an individual in the open eye (a big name, government official, or sports star, maybe). Sit and spotlight discreetly on the photograph. Note down any musings which come to you. Attempt to concentrate on getting data which you'll have the option to confirm, for example, where/when this individual was conceived, regardless of whether they have kin or where they live at this point. At that point, you can check your data and perceive how close you were.

4. Search for Auras

Each living thing has a quality, and it's a great psychic practice to check whether you can recognize it. This is most straightforward when the subject is against a pale foundation – basically gaze marginally around the individual, creature, or pot plant (on the off chance that you don't have co-employable family or companions!), and in the long run, you will begin to make out fluffy hues and tones. The more you practice, the simpler this will turn into.

5. Analysis with Cards

Tarot cards and prophet decks of various types are phenomenal for creating psychic mindfulness. Pick a couple of packs that advance to you, and simply play with them. You can take a stab at giving basic readings, if you like, or simply work with each card in turn and look actually profoundly to attempt to instinctively comprehend the imagery on the card. Regardless of whether you need to pursue the translations from a manual, don't be reluctant to give your psychic personality a chance to make jumps and associations – the main thing is the manner by which you see the cards, not how the creator saw them.

Effective Methods to Develop Psychic Abilities: Exercises to Try

#1: Meditate Daily for 10-15 Minutes

Raising your body's vibration is a significant part of building up your psychic capacities. This is because otherworldly vitality vibrates at a higher recurrence. Ruminating normally will enable you to be loose and raise your vitality vibration. Over the long haul, you will start to feel an expanded association with your Higher Self, Spirit, and others' vitality. If you get exhausted from your commonplace contemplation, attempt guided reflections.

#2: Learn About Your Spirit Guides

If you seek after the psychic way, at that point, your soul aides will be there to help you each progression en route – so it's imperative to acquaint yourself with them and become more acquainted with them – you particularly need to figure out how to confide in them. While you are ruminating, request that your aides uncover themselves to you around then. Ask them what their names are. Try not to sift anything through; simply go with it and trust what you see.

#3: Practice Psychometry Skills

Psychometry alludes to perusing the vitality of an article. This is fun and is an extraordinary technique to begin rehearsing in your capacities. Basically, start by holding an item – particularly a metal article and something with a great deal of vitality, similar to a wedding band – and shut your eyes to check whether you can naturally observe, sense, or hear anything about the item's proprietor.

#4: Develop Your Clairvoyance with Flower Visualization

This is a particularly fun method! You start by shutting your eyes and concentrating on your third eye region. At that point, welcome your Spirit Guides to indicate you quiet pictures of excellence and be missing some other idea. Allow your mind to meander, and the pictures will normally flood your third eye!

#5: Take a Nature Walk

Contemplation shouldn't exhaust or be done while sitting. You can appreciate a care reflection by going for a nature stroll. Focus on each progression as you walk and spotlight on your body's development. With each progression, rehash "step." This will help you in clearing your third eye from mess and will likewise build your vibration. Indeed, even a customary nature walk is likewise amazingly reflective!

#6: Read Psychic Development Books

Perusing causes you to turn out to be progressively mindful of your abilities, so perusing a couple of pages of a psychic advancement book day by day will assist you with learning increasingly about your regular gifts and sharpen your aptitudes as you learn.

#7: Visit an Antique Store

These stores are loaded with vitality. Visit an old-fashioned store and focus on what you instinctively sense and feel when you are in the store! Does the vitality feel overwhelming? Great? Get various articles and see what you sense. Possibly you'll hear a name or see a dream!

#8: Make a Symbol Book

Frequently, psychic data comes to us in various manners. It regularly has a representative quality and shouldn't be taken truly. Your Spirit Guides will help you in translating things as your psychic capacities create. Get a diary and pen you like and sit unobtrusively while you welcome your Angels and Spirit Guides to support you. Request that they demonstrate to you an image, for example, for occasions and occupations. For instance, they may demonstrate to you a birthday cake to speak to a birthday, or you may hear the glad birthday tune. Compose these down in your image book, so later, if you are demonstrated that image once more, you will recollect what it implies.

#9: Practice Your Aura-Seeing Skills

Anybody can figure out how to see qualities, and it happens to be an extraordinary method to build up your psychic aptitudes. Have a companion remain before a divider with plain shading. Venture back eight feet. At that point, center on their temple (third eye territory) and envision you are glancing through them, at the divider past. You will start to see the air layer around their head.

#10: Practice Giving Readings Often

The most ideal approach to build up expertise at something is to practice, and it's a vital aspect for turning into a medium or psychic. Give readings each shot you get and watch your expertise, exactness, and certainty increment with each perusing.

#11: Tune-in to Your Pet

At the point when your pet is quiet, have a go at sitting with the person in question and instinctively getting on their emotions. This builds up your clairsentience.

#12: Try Reading Old Family Photos

An image says a thousand words – and would you be able to peruse those words from an image utilizing your natural capacities and psychic endowments? Take a gander at individuals in old photographs and write everything down that you sense from them. This is a fun method to build up your psychic abilities!

#13: Journal Often

Visit journaling causes you to check out your higher self, your spirit, and your otherworldly aides. Take a stab at thinking about a circumstance that you could utilize some direction. Diary about it and enable yourself to unwind and be supernaturally guided simultaneously.

#14: Join a Spiritual Development Circle or Class

Nobody is ever enough of a specialist at something that they don't have anything to gain from others. Have a go at taking a class or joining a psychic advancement hover to meet others on their otherworldly adventure and see what you can get from them!

#15: Focus Your Third Eye

Hyper vision is one of the essential capacities that accompany being psychic. To create it, take a couple of minutes to concentrate on your third eye region, which lies simply above and between your eyebrows. Envision your third educational. If you do, you may even feel the spot start to shiver!

Chapter Five

Advantages of Meditation for Psychic Development

Contemplation and psychic advancement

When you're chipping away at building up your psychic aptitudes – from hyper vision to rune or Tarot perusing – the establishment to everything is your capacity to tune in and focus on whatever you are getting.

Each of us is a part of the last piece of the inestimable web or quantum field. Any psychic aptitude is extremely about interfacing with all that there is – all that you're as of now part of! However, the huge issue is that we truly overwhelm our association with our regular musings and the quick furor of everyday life.

Reflection is a splendid method to figure out how to calm your brain down so you can psychically tune in and experience that inestimable association freely.

Each and every profound custom, from antiquated to current, contains a type of contemplation practice, and it is one more region where science and otherworldliness concur on the advantages.

In only one of the examinations done at the University of Wisconsin, Tibetan priests were wired up during reflection, and it was found that contemplation produced an increase in gamma waves around the left prefrontal cortex – a zone, unexpectedly, likewise connected with bliss and nice sentiments.

Reflection has been demonstrated to have the option to truly revamp our cerebrums for satisfaction, and this gets an entire host of advantages in its wake.

In any case, with regards to helping us build up our psychic aptitudes, reflection likewise causes us still the brain and chop down the prattle of our ordinary musings. When we can enable our brain to go calm, we are unquestionably progressively responsive to the data that we can psychically tune into utilizing whatever apparatuses help us center our expectations.

So as the old joke goes, when you are attempting to build up your psychic abilities, don't simply accomplish something – stay there. The more that you can clear your brain, the better you will have the option to check out the enormous web. Finding that spot of harmony inside your own brain could be the missing piece to making the quantum jump in your psychic capacities.

Some significant advantages of reflections for psychic improvement are:

Control Your Mind

Maybe the most significant explanation reflection is significant for psychic advancement is so you can control your brain. When you are getting data for other individuals from your aides and higher energies, you don't need that errant idea about expecting to make the clothing slip into your head and divert you.

The demonstration of getting data in itself is an unobtrusive move in vitality. You should know and focus, so the significant data doesn't go by without you taking notes. A few impressions can last just a millisecond, and you don't need that data to be lost since you began pondering what to prepare for supper.

I have discovered that the fundamental routine with regards to following your broadness to be the most ideal approach to figure out how to control your psyche thusly. Simply attempt it at the present time and perceive how troublesome it is. Take a stab at taking in and out for ten adjusts and see where your mind winds up. Hard, isn't it! This strategy takes practice and can be disappointing; however, it is the most flawlessly awesome in figuring out how to assume responsibility for your psyche.

Know Yourself

Another significant motivation to ruminate is with the goal that you can become acquainted with what considerations in your psyche are originating from you and which are originating from your aides. The most ideal approach to do this is to invest some quality energy with yourself and just yourself.

When you are chipping away at following your expansiveness, what sorts of things are striking a chord? Who is this inward you that you have been disregarding for such a long time? By becoming acquainted with that one-of-a-kind vitality that is all your very own, you will have the option to know when an alternate vitality is coming into your mindfulness.

Raise Your Vibration

Contemplation can likewise assist you with raising your vibration. Am I not catching this' meaning? We are all vitality and live in this lower vitality world. Those "on the opposite side" or your aides and heavenly attendants work at a much higher vitality level. In order to speak with them viably, we should figure out how to raise our vibrations while they bring down their vibrations, so we can compromise.

Contemplation is one such technique that we can use to enable us to raise our vibrations. Simply quieting the psyche and concentrating on your expansiveness, you will before long end up having all the more cherishing contemplations and encounters. Love has a higher vibrational recurrence than stress and dread, and by focusing on this affection, you will raise your vibration too.

Normal Meditation Benefits

Notwithstanding the particular psychic advantages of reflection, the more normally gushed motivations to ponder are additionally significant for that maturing psychic. One reason contemplation is becoming so well-known is its capacity to help decrease pressure. There are such a large number of logical investigations out there clarifying precisely how contemplation quiets the brain and helps quiet the body. Schools are currently, in any event, beginning to execute reflection to enable understudies to figure out how to all the more likely control their conduct. Furthermore, any psychic in the field realizes that holding their feelings of anxiety under control encourages readings to be clearer and more heart-focused.

Interface with Your Higher Self

Did you realize that there would someone say someone is who knows precisely for what reason you're here and what your life's calling is? No, there's not a genuine Yoda. It's your Higher Self.

And keeping in mind that it would be excessively advantageous to shoot your Higher Self a Facebook message, the most ideal approach to speak with that infinitely knowledgeable piece of you is through reflection.

When we reflect, we plunge profound and center around ourselves. Since our Higher Self is the profound side of us, reflection brings us thereby sheer definition.

Dispose of Nasty Energy

This is outstanding amongst other reflection benefits ever!

Much the same as our homes need occasional profound cleans, so do our vitality fields! Reflection resembles Mrs. Meyers for our vitality.

It enables us to clear out the inner spider webs, expel ourselves from every day, and refocus on what's significant.

Doing that not only kicks negative vitality to the control, it also raises our vibe, which welcomes it might be said of harmony and calmness that no dreadful vitality needs to be near.

Accomplish Better Emotional Balance

This is very significant when you are on an otherworldly voyage or building up your psychic capacities (once more, since it keeps your vibration high).

Contemplation helps wipe the record of past encounters clean and let you consider them to be as it is today.

This new viewpoint advances passionate equalization and enables you to acquaint your intelligent self with your otherworldly self!

Increment Spiritual Health

Contemplation removes us from being overpowered and enables us to just watch... it practically powers the present on you (positively)!

By placing ourselves in an observer perspective (observing as opposed to connecting with contemplations), we can begin to return to the present minute (otherwise called care), offer our mind a reprieve, and recover our otherworldly wellbeing.

Increment Your Intuition

Our instinct is correspondence from the non-physical piece of us (otherwise known as our Higher Self/soul) and our otherworldly group!

It's what instructs you to not eat that frank from the corner store, what your mother truly needs for her birthday, and that the more interesting you just met is dependable.

Since reflection carries us closer to our Higher Self, it enables us to get increasingly more receptive to our instinct.

The most effective method to Meditate

Clearly, you need to get in on a portion of those previously mentioned contemplation benefits... so we should dive into how to really reflect!

- Sit in a comfortable spot and pop your earphones in.
- Try to maintain your attention exclusively on the guided contemplation.
- If your mind begins to wander, delicately take it back to the guide.

Tip: Don't get debilitated if your mind continues meandering that is absolutely ordinary from the start. Contemplation resembles making meatballs – it gets simpler each time you do it.

Discretionary contemplation enhancers:

- Essential oil diffuser (take a stab at diffusing lavender, lemon, rose, or frankincense)

- Salt light
- Journal and pen (I profoundly prescribe journaling after reflection!)
- Cozy pads and covers (reflection ought to be comfortable)
- Meditation (mala) dabs
- An individual mantra

Reflection Benefits Takeaways

There's no set-in-stone manner to ruminate. Yippee!

Some reflection advantages include expanded instinct, more grounded psychic capacities, and passionate equalization!

Contemplation additionally supports your vibe and enables you to kick negative vitality to the check. It gets out old sentiments and decisions and enables you to have a glossy, new point of view. It additionally enables you to associate with your Higher Self and Spiritual Guides.

Chapter Six

Types of Psychic Development

Clairaudience is the capacity of getting a natural vocal message from the universe of spirits or a higher being. Clairaudient individuals can stretch out their hearing to rise above the ordinary physical world and the known degree of mindfulness so as to arrive at the world past. Clairaudients are profoundly natural individuals who can tune in to a voice other than their own when the soul world transmits a message to them.

The message may incorporate specific words, names or expressions, incoherent sounds, or music. The voice now and then sounds incredibly unique in relation to the voices we typically hear. It might seem as though it's being spoken right by you, inside your head, or resounding as though from another measurement. It likewise may seem like one of your friends and family who has passed away. The voice may make itself heard now and again of an emergency, a crisis, an intersection, or at another huge time. Clairaudient dreams are additionally a known wonder, where an individual may hear the voice of a soul during rest.

How does clairaudience sound?

Clairaudience is normally heard inside (in your mind).

Some of the time, clairaudient messages can be heard with your "customary hearing." However, recall – those in the Spirit world never again have a physical body – in this manner, needn't bother with a physical "voice."

Tip: If you need to be an expert instinctive, clairaudience can be too useful to create. Then again, if psychic hearing isn't your most grounded instinctive blessing, no stress! You mustn't have each "clair" all the way open so as to be a stunning instinctive!

Ways You Can Receive Clairaudient Messages

1. You hear YOUR very own voice in your mind

Clairaudience is delicate and unobtrusive. It regularly seems like when you are contemplating internally.

For instance, in case I'm doing mediumship perusing and my customer's Uncle Joe is speaking with me by means of my clairaudience, I don't hear the voice Uncle Joe had while he was alive. I hear him in my voice, in my mind.

Consider it a clairvoyant method for imparting.

When you've built up this natural blessing, you'll have the option to separate between your own voice and the voice of Spirit, as well.

2. Sounds

You may hear sounds, words, or music in your mind. They may have exacting or representative implications.

In case I'm giving a perusing and Spirit needs me to realize they as of late had a birthday, I may hear the Happy Birthday tune in my mind.

3. Physical Sounds from the Ether

On uncommon events, you may hear words, music, or sounds remotely with your standard hearing – yet there is no hotspot for the sound.

At some point, my back rub specialist and I started hearing the most excellent music, yet there was nobody else in the structure and no radios around! We could both hear this ethereal music with our ordinary hearing.

Envision how cool that would be if that happened constantly. We'd spare a fortune on iTunes!

4. The voice of Spirit

Most mediums hear Spirit clairvoyantly in their very own voice. Be that as it may, here and there, the voice of Spirit will seem as it did while they were living.

The first run through this transpired, I could unmistakably hear my companion's sister in Spirit saying the name John. It was astounding! I had the option to portray her voice and the manner in which she articulated her words.

These kinds of clairaudient encounters are sure and not unnerving.

5. Clairaudient alerts

If an individual is in trouble and their soul group needs to stand out enough to be noticed immediately, they MAY hear a clairaudient cautioning unmistakably.

This marvel isn't intended to be alarming; however, it can be frightening (this is another motivation behind why Spirit likes to speak with delicate, clairvoyant messages).

Furthermore, trust me, if your otherworldly group ensures you by shouting "STOP," you'll be overly appreciative they did!

Where Do Clairaudient Messages Come From?

When you are far enough along in your psychic improvement, you'll start to get a feeling of who is sending you a message and why.

- It may be from your Spirit Guides
- It could be from somebody you adore who's passed on
- It could be from your Higher Self

Signs You Might be Clairaudient

There are numerous clairaudient individuals strolling around this world who don't realize they have this super-cool instinctive blessing. Is it safe to say that you are one of them?

1. Hear somebody saying your name when nobody is near

Does it ever appear as though you hear individuals talking, yet nobody is near? Perhaps you hear delicate voices out of sight or could have SWORN you heard somebody saying your name.

If this transpires, it's a pretty darn great pointer that you might be clairaudient.

When you have psychic hearing, you can now and again hear things that other individuals can't. It might be a delicate, unpretentious sound (like music) or something increasingly emotional (like a voice).

2. You appreciate and need calm

Instinctive individuals are generally exceptionally delicate, both genuinely and physically. Along these lines, you might be touchy to clamor in case you're clairaudient.

For instance, a noisy gathering or TV may make you feel – goodness – like you are going to slither out of your skin! By and by, this is my solitary protest about being clairaudient.

A lot of commotion may make you feel:

- tired
- irritable
- ungrounded
- or give you a cerebral pain

It tends to be truly disappointing when you have psychic hearing; however, your loved ones don't see the amount it influences you.

3. You converse with yourself frequently

Do you have discussions with yourself in your mind ALL the time? It could imply that clairaudience is one of your overwhelming instinctive endowments. Why?

All things considered since you are as of now great at "being in your mind", it will be simple for you to figure out how to perceive when you're taken advantage of Spirit.

If you converse with yourself a great deal, you're most likely getting Divine direction without acknowledging it!

4. Thoughts and inventiveness move through you

In case you're clairaudient, you may have numerous inventive, enlivened thoughts that course through you — particularly when you are feeling loose, euphoric, or thankful.

This is because when you are cheerful, your vibration is high, and you are most associated with your spirit!

This is the reason clairaudient individuals look for calm. We instinctively realize that in that isolation, we can interface with the Divine.

It's even regular for individuals with psychic hearing to get bunches of motivated thoughts while cleaning up! I propose bath colored pencils, so you don't miss any of the directions you get.

5. Your closest companions were nonexistent

Contrarily! "Fanciful" companions can be heavenly attendants, Spirit directs, and even withdrawn friends and family.

If you conversed with a fanciful companion as a youngster, either clairvoyantly or on the off chance that you heard a physical voice, you are presumably clairaudient.

6. Music makes you feel associated with your spirit

Recently, Tom Petty was on TV discussing how music originates from the spirit.

When you focused on it, it's generally because your spirit needs something, and you're not tuning in. That is the point at which you get in your vehicle, jump on the closest nation street, and play the music that you cherish! Inside only a couple of minutes, your vibration is lifted, and you feel reconnected to your spirit.

If music moves you to this degree, you might be clairaudient.

You may likewise be:

- Musically slanted or improvise
- Write music – You may "hear" the music before you compose it, or it might feel propelled by a higher power

On a side note… if you start seeing pictures in your mind to coordinate the melody verses, it might likewise mean you are extrasensory!

7. You Lift Others Up

- Do you appreciate managing and elevating others?
- Do individuals reveal to you that you should charge cash for offering guidance or that you have a "blessing"?
- Do individuals call you to "vent" since your words are so alleviating?

8. Hear ringing or shrill commotions in your ears

You may likewise hear humming or feel your ears "pop." If it's too noisy, it's OK to state, hello folks, cut back the volume!

9. You learn through the sound-related channel

Your favored method for learning can be a piece of information with respect to which psychic blessings you have. Numerous clairaudient individuals adapt best through hearing. Or on the other hand, you may appreciate tuning in to a book on Audible as opposed to perusing a book.

10. You can "hear" creatures

Hearing creatures doesn't mean they open their mouths and start visiting like Mr. Ed or anything; it's progressively similar to "squares of an idea" that fly into your head.

For instance, I was petting my feline one day when an idea flew into my head that my little girl has been disclosing our kitty privileged insights! I referenced this to my girl, and she yelled, "He did! Did he reveal to you what my mystery is?" He didn't. Shucks for me.

11. You get "signs" in melody and discourse

Signs can make you feel associated with Spirit, feel approved, and are a TON of enjoyable to search for! Signs from Spirit can come to us in every single way.

If you request a sign from your aides or friends and family in paradise, pay heed to how they come through for you.

Does the direction you've been looking for come through in the following tune that plays on the radio? Or, on the other hand, do you end up saying, "Entertaining you should state that," when a more bizarre says precisely what you have to hear? Provided that this is true, these are attributes of clairaudience.

Types of Psychic Awareness (b)

CLAIRCOGNIZANCE

Claircognizance is unmistakable, profound knowledge. It is the inclination you get when you instinctively realize what you have to do. Numerous individuals experience such minutes, alluding to them as a premonition or inward assurance.

Claircognizance regularly happens when we get outsiders who end together turning into our dearest companions or sentimental accomplices. The association is a moment: You feel as though you definitely know the individual, and there's no feeling of ungainliness between you.

Claircognizant individuals may encounter more than one psychic capacity. This implies because somebody is claircognizant, it doesn't imply that they can't likewise be clairaudient. It is conceivable to have each of the four instinctive faculties as one distinctive individual.

It tends to be hard to recognize a hunch and claircognizance. Numerous individuals have senses that may lead them the correct way, yet those with the endowment of claircognizance can know things reliably with no proof at all.

They can be reliably right with regards to expectations about future occasions or bits of knowledge into goals or the reality of a circumstance.

Have you at any point had a premonition that let you know not to accept a position offer or known in a split second that a choice you had would affect an amazing remainder? These are instances of claircognizant knowing. This is an awesome type of instinct in case you're continually settling on snappy choices, and numerous fruitful specialists are exceptionally taken advantage of their claircognizant capacities, regardless of whether they know.

Figuring out how to interface with this type of instinct is an awesome method to begin building up your psychic capacities. Next time you get a sentiment of all-out assurance with respect to your affection life, vocation, or another individual issue, observe it. Record it in your diary and record the sensation and feeling that accompanied it. This basic demonstration of believing your hunch will open the entryway to interfacing with and using your claircognizant capacities

Here are a few markers that you may have claircognizance:

Right Gut Instincts

We as a whole as people have impulses. A portion of these impulses originate from the manner in which we were raised and our past experience, some come hereditarily, and some come because of profound associations. These gut impulses, if essentially dependent on past experience, are not in every case right.

The intuition to not confide in pooches since one hurt you as a youngster is a sense that is significant and legitimate, however not constantly right. Few out of every odd canine is rough.

For somebody with claircognizance, however, senses and premonitions are an endowment of truth. In spite of never having met their companion's date for the evening or heard anything besides beneficial things about him, somebody with claircognizance may have a negative premonition about him. If so, it will at that point turn out later that he wasn't extremely kind on the date, or perhaps he even stood her up.

This capacity to nearly anticipate occasions dependent on a gut "knowing" feeling and being reliably demonstrated right by the result is the thing that makes claircognizance such a blessing to the individuals who have it. If your gut impulses are constantly demonstrated genuine, you may have the endowment of claircognizance.

You Can Always Spot a Liar

Regardless of how incredible this young lady is or how kind your colleague is being, on the off chance that you have claircognizance, you can generally detect a harmless embellishment. In any event, when somebody is essentially being unscrupulous with their feelings or articulations of feeling, somebody with claircognizance can see these deceptions.

It is simple for the individuals throughout your life to confide in your recommendations or thoughts regarding individuals if you are claircognizant due to your capacity to realize whether individuals are coming clean or not has been demonstrated valid again and again.

If the sentiment of realizing that somebody is being insincere or intentionally false keeps on being demonstrated genuine later, and if those sentiments of knowing depended on premonitions instead of real proof and physical faculties, at that point, you are in all likelihood encountering the endowments of being a claircognizant person.

You Receive Messages as Random Ideas or Solutions

Somebody with the endowment of claircognizance as a psychic capacity will every so often have reality dawned on you through an abrupt, apparently arbitrary idea or thought. These can be thoughts as straightforward as "I should check the locks on my vehicle" or "My gathering tomorrow will be dropped."

If finishing these contemplations winds up keeping you from genuine results or repercussions, at that point, you may have the endowment of claircognizance. This implies you may not know when these messages will come in or precisely what they mean constantly, yet when they do come, it is a smart thought to watch them and to guarantee that whatever your gut is attempting to caution you about is kept from occurring.

Awakening with an answer for an issue is another pointer of claircognizance, as it demonstrates that your gut is working in any event when your mind isn't. Without proof expected to discover an answer, your gut can know the response to the issue. This is the quintessential capacity related to claircognizance.

You Are Able to Predict Events

Past the rationale and proof of a given circumstance, claircognizant people who were given the psychic endowment of instinctive faculties just as physical ones can know the result of a circumstance regularly before the circumstance happens or gives enough physical proof to gather the result.

Most basic leadership and end drawing have originated from physical proof dependent on physical faculties like sight or smell. With claircognizance, however, it is conceivable to settle on educated choices about the result regarding a circumstance without this proof. These people can just know.

If you have ever entered a circumstance with gut learning of the result, just to find that your gut information was right, you may have the capacity of claircognizance. Knowing the aftereffects of a test or test, having an inclination about a companion's wellbeing, or anticipating a significant life occasion for somebody are largely extraordinary instances of this capacity in real life.

Knowing what's to come is absurd with the five physical faculties; however, it is with claircognizance. Those with this capacity can make inductions dependent on premonitions and impulses that, as a general rule, end up being valid.

Types of Psychic Awareness

Hyper vision

What is Clairvoyance?

Special insight is a French word that signifies "Clear Seeing." It's a psychic capacity, the sixth natural Sense, and the unobtrusive observation that enables us to see vitality. We have our typical 5 faculties of the body (contact, taste, locate, smell, hearing), and we additionally have numerous psychic detects that the soul uses to get increasingly unpretentious data past the five conventional faculties.

Perceptiveness works with your Spiritual Eye, as opposed to the physical eyes. The profound eye is the sixth Chakra or Third Eye, and it is a vitality focus in the mid-cerebrum, behind the temple.

Chakra is a Sanskrit word that signifies "wheel" or "vitality focus". A chakra resembles a turning wheel of light and vitality. Chakras contain our profound data. They help the soul procedure data, much like the five detects process data for the body. The soul gets data utilizing a wide range of chakras, and each chakra has a profound or psychic capacity. Perceptiveness is the Spiritual capacity of the sixth chakra.

What's the Difference between "Psychic" and "Perceptiveness"?

Hyper vision is a "psychic" capacity, and there are a lot of increasingly psychic capacities notwithstanding Clairvoyance.

You could consider "psychic" to be an expansive term, similar to the word nourishment. There are zillions of kinds of nourishment; the equivalent goes with sorts of psychic encounters. Nourishment may mean a couple of leaves picked from the correct plant, inexpensive food, or an eight-course dinner. It could mean vegetables, frozen yogurt, pasta, popcorn, natural product serving of mixed greens, chocolate, kimchee, green curry - there is an apparently perpetual rundown of nourishment potential outcomes, and each gives an altogether different encounter and diverse healthful or synthetic impacts.

We have a soul body and a physical body.

The psychic fields are similarly as wide. The psychic experience incorporates everything from Clairvoyance (clear observing) to clairvoyance (hearing correspondence without somebody standing up noisy), to directing (bringing a soul into your body) to clairsentience (feeling what another person feels), thus substantially more!

"Psychic" originates from the Greek, and it signifies "Soul Personality Energy." All of us have soul character vitality. This is the vitality of a soul. It's what rises above material presence and enables us to be quite a lot more. Soul character vitality contains the whole magical domain. We each likewise have "body character vitality." Body character vitality is identified with existence, and it's this vitality that enables us to deal with our regular nuts and bolts.

We have both body and soul, and it's significant that we care for every one of them so we can be dynamically sound, lavishly alive, and conscious of our actual profound way. A large number of us are shown a few nuts and bolts dealing with the body (eat healthily, get some activity, rest is significant, etc.!). However, what number of us are instructed how to think about our spirit in a supporting, regarding way? Psychic preparing gives you apparatuses and assets to tune in to the requirements of your spirit and feed your soul.

Since you have a spirit and soul character vitality, this implies you are psychic! You don't need to figure out how to end up a psychic – you, as of now, are psychic! To intentionally utilize your psychic capacities, you simply need to practice the muscle and get out the convictions and thoughts that shield you from knowing and getting your profound truth. It's a procedure of "recalling" your inalienable capacity!

At the Clairvoyant Center of Hawaii, we show individuals how to practice the muscle of their characteristic Clairvoyance and to create psychic mindfulness utilizing the Third Eye.

Signs that You're a Clairvoyant Psychic

If special insight is one of your natural blessings, you may:

- Have mental pictures arbitrarily streak before your eyes
- Find it simple to picture places, individuals, and so forth.
- See flashes of hues, numbers, images, or pictures
- Sometimes appear as though a "motion picture" is playing in your mind

Visual psychic flashes — No, you're not going bonkers. Flashes of shading and light can now and again be your Spirit Guides or different individuals from your profound family. You may see:

- Floating circles or hued "masses" are noticeable all around
- Glowing light around individuals (their quality)
- Shadows that appear as though they are skimming noticeable all around
- Glittering or glimmering lights are noticeable all around
- Movement or twinkling lights out of the edge of your eyes

Dream effectively – Because special insight has to do with seeing, representation is a HUGE piece of it.

For instance, in case you're a visionary psychic, it would be simple for you to envision tasting Sangria while sitting on the seashore in Maui, wearing Birkenstocks and red Foster Grant shades.

You can find in your mind how something ought to be with the goal that it "works" right – Like when you purchase a household item at Ikea, and it takes the normal individual 10 hours to assemble it due to the fact that there are 5,000 pieces; however, you can whip that child together in two hours… you can perceive how it should all fit together.

You have an extraordinary ability to know east from west – You're a human GPS. Siri approaches you for headings.

Complete visual-spatial errands effectively – Like finishing a labyrinth in a riddle book or perusing a guide.

Attracted to occupations and interests that energize you outwardly – An extrasensory psychic may examine home-enhancing web journals on a Sunday morning or be attracted to a vocation as an inside originator or greens keeper.

Acknowledge wonderful things – Clairvoyant psychics truly acknowledge excellence. You may venerate artistic work, photography, or home style.

Step by step instructions to Improve Your Clairvoyant Psychic Abilities

Expanding your extrasensory blessings is simpler — and most likely substantially more fun — than you suspected conceivable!

Fundamentally, it's much the same as adapting some other ability. Practice and persistence are what is required. Invest energy in these interests and unwind:

- Meditate
- Visualizing
- Open your Third Eye Chakra

Different Forms of Psychic Abilities

Remember that special insight is only one of the numerous kinds of psychic capacities. There are various others, including empaths, mediumship, and instinct.

You may have heard "medium" utilized during discourses about psychic capacities, especially those including correspondence with the soul world. Customarily, a medium is somebody who talks, somehow, to the dead.

For certain individuals, psychic capacity shows as psychic compassion. Empaths can detect the sentiments and feelings of others without their letting us know.

Instinct is the capacity to simply *know* things without being told. Numerous intuitive persons make magnificent Tarot card readers since this ability gives them a preferred position while perusing cards for a customer. This is once in a while alluded to as clairsentience.

Learn Telepathy

Clairvoyance is only one kind of psychic work. For this clairvoyance practice, you will require an accomplice. Attempt to discover an accomplice who is near you, for example, family or dear companion and somebody with a receptive outlook and who has an uplifting disposition. Choose who will be the collector and who will be the sender for this activity. The collector will be the one getting the picture, word, or whatever the sender needs to send.

Before doing this activity, you most likely need to do basic breathing or establishing reflection exercises to persuade your brain to be peaceful and your body to be without a care in the world and prepared for your psychic exercise. It will be simpler to get outside impressions if your brain is still and void of musings.

Clairvoyance Exercise

Stage 1

Sit before one another on seats with the two feet level on the ground to make a sentiment of being grounded. Close your eyes and take two or three seconds to settle with a couple of profound personality loosening up breaths. Open your eyes and investigate the individual before you get an unmistakable mental perception of the landscape and where the other individual sits. You may wish to concentrate on the temple of the other individual, as that is the place you will center when sending the representation.

Stage 2

Presently close your eyes. Presently the sender must begin to send the picture the person has chosen to send. You can pick an image, word, sound, feeling, and so on., yet it might be simpler, to begin with, an image since it might be simpler to imagine as you send it. Select an image with an unmistakable shading or shape.

Stage 3

Picture a channel of vitality gradually moving out of your brow and ends up more grounded and more and moves towards the recipients' temple. Picture the vitality trench, become one with the recipient's brow, and there will presently be a vitality channel between you. Presently, take the picture you need to send and make it truly clear in your brain. Envision that you are sending the picture from your psyche and through the passage towards the recipient, take as much time as necessary, and don't surge it. Picture it gradually arriving at the collector's brow and afterward infiltrate their brain. See the picture as plainly as you can in the psyche of the beneficiary and keep on doing as such. Give the other individual a chance to disclose to you what the person in question saw with however many subtleties as could be expected under the circumstances.

Chapter Seven

Utilizing Psychic Ability to Levitate

Levitation is the capacity to ascend from the beginning the psychic capacity of the brain. It is conceivable to prepare yourself to accomplish levitation equivalent to it is conceivable to build up any of your psychic capacities through preparing. The mind takes in everything that it experiences regardless of whether you don't intentionally enroll it. What's more, this is as valid for the otherworldly world all things considered of the physical world. Preparing yourself to utilize your inborn capacities is tied in with getting more in contact with the profound side and inclining to raise it from an oblivious to a conscious level. This should be possible with focus and cautious preparation.

There are numerous strategies that you may run over for figuring out how to suspend. If you can outfit your natural psychic capacity and create it in a suitable manner, then levitation ought to be inside your domain of conceivable outcomes. The clearest thing about levitation would appear to be the capacity to ascend from the beginning; this is really not the best spot to begin. It is absolutely not the thing to concentrate on if you want to succeed. The most significant thing is to focus on clearing your mind and connecting with the otherworldly world. You can prepare to do this and increment your capacities to an exceptionally elevated level.

Thus, the initial phase in physical levitation is to not stress over whether you will succeed, yet to focus on connecting your brain with the psychic measurement. If you can associate and have an uplifted consciousness of this association, at that point, you will be en route to effective levitation. Having the option to control your contemplations and effectively utilize the shrouded encounters of the mind will empower you to accomplish astonishing things. Levitation is conceivable through incredibly centered use of the vitality that you can center with the intensity of your psyche.

To accomplish fruitful levitation, you first need to accuse your group of psychic vitality. You should do this in your very own manner that you have prepared to do. After this, you can picture yourself remaining before your very own body. You, at that point, need to utilize your perception methods to see your vitality moving into your physical body and just now explicitly center on utilizing that vitality to suspend your body starting from the earliest stage. You should center the power moving through your psyche on lifting your body from the beginning spotlight just on the perception of this event. Hold the picture for a brief span; at that point, let your physical body tenderly come back to the ground. While you are on the right edge of awareness, rehash the levitation a few times on the off chance that you feel good with it.

In the beginning, it is critical to comprehend why creating and utilizing your psychic aptitudes is significant. We as a whole have capacities, for example, clairvoyance, special insight, ESP, and direct personality over issue control as psychokinesis. Psychokinesis is a significant psychic ability since it enables one to legitimately control matter with the brain. We can clearly perceive how this is so significant for all everyday issues, and particularly as far as showing whatever we may require when we need it and furthermore whatever we profoundly want.

We as a whole have expectations, dreams, and desires that we need to show, and for reasons unknown, there is generally blockage. This blockage is effectively expelled when we figure out how to utilize our psychic personality over mater powers. That is the subject of this article. The absolute best data that I can give on the best way to adequately utilize and control your psychic capacities are from my very own understanding. Presently, I've adapted the greater part of what I think about arousing and utilizing psychic capacities inside the setting of yoga, chakras, contemplation, and by working with the sacrosanct composition known as "PK."

That original copy is clearly probably the best asset for figuring out how to function with psychokinesis and brain over issue all in all. Psychokinesis, or "PK" is immediate personality over issue control. It empowers us to move objects a ways off, to control and show however a lot simpler, to impact results, normally recuperate ourselves as well as other people, and to effectively pull in whatever is required or profoundly wanted in your life. I'm sure you can perceive how this particular psychic capacity can be very beneficial.

Once more, we are generally clearly brought into the world with numerous psychic capacities. These include The capacity to astral venture into different universes, particularly during rest, show thought and goal, regular mending powers. It additionally incorporates powers, for example, mental clairvoyance, perceptiveness, and psychokinesis. Commonly these idle capacities in people are activated, stirred, and initiated because of specific practices and even by basically coming into contact with minor learning or data. For instance, numerous individuals have encountered extraordinary psychic or brain-over issues marvel following coming into contact with specific individuals, certain data, or after simply doing certain practices, for example, yoga, reflection, or chakra work.

The manners in which that our psychic capacities are activated or stirred depends to a great extent on our individual and novel Karma. Perhaps perusing this article or catching up with related data will stir and additionally improve your psychic capacities. Regardless, I can guarantee you that at whatever point you do encounter your genuine psychic PK control, you will know it, and you won't confuse it with whatever else. These capacities are genuine and also very fascinating to encounter. Besides yoga, chakras, and contemplation work, there are numerous different methodologies for promptly arousing and setting off our psychic capacities.

These capacities are critical to think about in light of the fact that they give one access to a totally different degree of mental and profound power. What's more, this influence influences our capacities throughout everyday life, our chances, and levels of favorable luck. Huge numbers of these methodologies are canvassed in the original copy. This Is PK and is very compelling. Our psychic abilities are ending up to a greater degree a basic instinct than all else. Solid instinct and internal learning are a higher priority than any time in recent memory in this age when we are, for the most part, being bombarded with so much data. These aptitudes can profit our lives in boundless manners. Actually, building up these higher capacities is the initial move towards living admirably in complete plenitude.

Once more, my favored technique for working with my own psychic capacities and creating them to the fullest is with yoga and reflection and chakra practice. I feel thusly for various great reasons. As a matter of first importance, yoga is one of the most seasoned and most solid frameworks for getting to our higher selves. The chakras are the most seasoned mapping arrangement of human instinct and potential. As I started working with mantra yoga and Bhakti yoga unto Lord Sri Krsna, my psychic capacities started thriving more than ever. It resembled a blossoming lotus blossom. PK is imperative to find out about the reason modern science pays attention to it very as a mind control that can control matter and even impact results by affecting the composition of "shot."

PK is associated with the quantum level of indication, and realizing how to depend individually close to home PK forces is the key to genuine individual freedom and boundless flourishing. Indeed, the study of psychokinesis has turned into a significant hotly debated issue among individuals from everywhere throughout the world since it uncovers reality with regards to what the intensity of our brains can do. It likewise has turned out to be such a hotly debated issue because numerous individuals out there, including me, have had individual encounters with PK and saw it direct. So normally, we look to know more and find out more, and we discover answers. After you realize that your PK power is genuine, at that point, you figure out how to utilize it and appreciate an actual existence loaded up with all that you have ever required and profoundly wanted. As I would like to think, the most ideal method for learning reality with regards to PK and how to function with your common psychic capacities is to gain from This Is PK composition and from your very own understanding.

How to Develop Psychic Abilities Effectively On Your Own

Psychic abilities are practical and useful. Clairvoyance allows you to see what your eyes cannot normally see. Clairaudience lets you hear; telepathy lets you communicate, and other psychic abilities let you perform other amazing tasks. Each of us is a psychic; it is just that not all of us know how to use our capabilities. If you wish to improve your life using these talents, then you have to know how to develop psychic abilities that lie dormant in you.

Learning

First and foremost, you need to learn more about psychic abilities. There are many books and guides you can read. The more knowledge you have about psychic abilities, the better your chances are of improving them.

Meditating

Meditating allows you to improve psychic abilities; moreover, it can also help you find peace and happiness. Various meditation methods can also be performed so you will become conscious of your mental states. You will also know how to distinguish psychic intuition from your everyday normal thoughts.

Praying

Prayer is necessary for asking for guidance or divine intervention for your goal to develop your psychic skills. Pray with the language of your heart and pray earnestly. Repeating the same prayers each night is not what you should do, but prayers that will express what your mind and heart really contain.

Affirming

Use affirmations every day so that your mind can be programmed to bring out the best outcomes. Affirmations are positive statements or suggestions that your subconscious mind can accept as true. Affirm to yourself that you have great powers to develop and that you are advancing well day after day.

Performing Rituals

Rituals are basically actions that you perform, which will have a corresponding effect on your inner plane. Rituals do not have to be as grave as what you see is done by wizards and witches. They could be just little things like praying while the hands are clasped together or candle lighting. No matter what ritual you perform, keep in mind that its core is to help you improve in your skills development.

Using Talisman

A talisman is an object held sacred for possessing some psychic charges. Any jewelry or stone can be used as a talisman. Crystals and other semi-precious stones like amethyst and jade can also be used. To use your chosen talisman, you need to clean it first using saltwater so that any impurity may be removed. After the cleansing, transfer your desire into the object. Wear this talisman every day in close contact with your skin.

Being With Other Psychics

When you are in the company of other people whose psychic abilities are developed, the more you will be inspired to be like them. Plus, they can also give you some helpful guidelines on how you can also improve your own skills. Their vibrations will help you get in tune with yours. You can attend seminars and workshops offered by other professional psychics. You can also search for online communities of people who share the same passion and interests in psychic abilities.

Believing

Another crucial component in developing your psychic powers is belief in yourself. If you are doubtful that you have powers, it would be impossible for you to prompt those powers to manifest. Even before you begin calling out for your abilities, you are already closing the doors where your powers will convene with you due to your certainty.

What is that special key for developing your psychic abilities? Well, it's dreaming. Believe it or not, dreams are a very powerful way to develop your psychic abilities, and you don't need to spend long hours in meditation or doing mental techniques. As a matter of fact, every night you go to sleep, you experience powerful psychic dreams. But because you do not understand what your dreams are trying to show you or understand how to program your dreams, you often overlook it as being nonsense. But dreams can be used in several ways as you're about to see.

There are a few ways of using your dreams to increase your psychic abilities, and one way of doing that is to begin to first understand what your dream symbols are trying to show you. That is the easiest part of psychic dreaming. Learning to understand the meaning of symbols helps to broaden your understanding of even simple fragmented dreams. Dreams that you would ordinarily consider as having no real meaning begin to open a whole new awareness once you understand the power of dream symbols.

Another way of using psychic dreams to increase your psychic abilities is to record every single detail that you can remember. Oftentimes, a dream may not have meaning to you, but over time as the day progresses, the dream begins to make more and more sense.

You begin to recognize the correlation between your dreams and your actual life experience. Writing your dreams down not only helps to increase your understanding, but you will begin to have proof that you are having dreams of events that will either happen in your life or somebody else's life. So, that is one essential tool to developing your psychic abilities, and that is to record every detail of your dreams.

Programming your dreams is another vital part of psychic dreaming that is so incredibly effective and powerful. Let us just imagine that you would like to get answers from a friend. You want to know if that person is being honest with you. Or, you want to know what that person is really like. All you need to do is to program your dreams so that you can enter into that person's energetic state. And when you enter that person's energetic state, you can inquire about anything that you want about that person. You can gain access to who that person is. And what that person thinks and feels about you, or any situation that you would like to get answers on. There is no limit to this sort of information that you can get using dreams as a vehicle to develop your psychic abilities.

Sorts of Psychic Abilities Quizzes

So how would you tell if you have psychic capacities or not? One path is with a psychic capacities test. There are two kinds of tests. Both have points of interest and weaknesses.

The principal type includes cards with images on them (traditionally circles, squares, and so on). Your assignment is to anticipate which image comes straightaway. This sort of test has been broadly utilized in ESP testing and has been around since the 1970s.

The fundamental issue with this test is that it basically depends on hyper-vision to find the right solution. Special insight or "clear observing" is a great psychic aptitude utilized by numerous psychic readers to foresee your future. Be that as it may, it is just one of the different sorts of ESP (or extra-tactile discernment). The other two principal types are clairaudience and clairsentience. Clairaudience (or "clear hearing") is the capacity to get inconspicuous messages by hearing, while clairsentience (or "clear feeling") is the capacity to associate with others with your emotions.

The second sort of test depends on recognizing certain individual attributes and encounters that may anticipate the nearness of psychic capacity. The primary weakness of this kind of test is that a few people guarantee that it isn't logical. Furthermore, I surmise that is valid - it doesn't give you a distinct score or a yes/no answer. In any case, from my perspective, psychic capacities are neither high contrast, nor would they be able to be evaluated enough by logical methods. So this kind of test is a subjective (rather than quantitative) type in a logical language. Or then again, at the end of the day, this sort of psychic capacities test is a right-brained test.

This sort has a few points of interest contrasted with the exemplary card-based ESP test. Right off the bat, it can distinguish a lot more extensive scope of psychic capacity (contingent upon the inquiry configuration), including the "huge three" talked about above, yet in addition supernatural power, profound direction, and clear imagining. Furthermore, it takes into account (and even depends on) the fluffiness that exists in the psychic world - the obscuring of outskirts between the nearness or nonattendance of psychic capacities. Furthermore, thirdly, it enables you to quantify your advancement after some time - by stepping through a similar examination at different interims during the advancement of your psychic aptitudes, you can check your improvement.

Chapter Eight

Tools For An Empath's Energy Protection

Empaths are attracted to recuperating themselves as well as other people. They are typically attracted to recuperating due to the fact that they feel that they have a lot of inner mending to do... until they understand that the majority of the recuperating required is for other people that they are instinctively 'feeling'.

They are ordinarily in a condition of steady weariness. This is a colossal issue. Individuals, alongside their energies, are always attacking an Empath's vitality. An Empath will, as a rule, take on something over the top and become depleted rapidly, and it's not effectively restored by rest or rest. It goes a lot further than that and is very debilitating.

Empaths are great audience members. They truly care about the prosperity of others and end up tuning in to the misfortunes of individuals they don't have a clue about. The vast majority discover Empaths so natural to open up to. That is the point at which they start dumping a wide range of cynicism going in their life. Here and there, individuals aren't even mindful they are doing this.

As a rule, an Empath will deal with the necessities of others even before their own because they care to such an extent. Since individuals get settled enough around them to open up, they will, as a rule, sacrificially listen closely to enable an individual, regardless of whether it's to their own hindrance.

Alone time is a need for Empaths. Numerous Empaths like to escape from the majority of the feelings and vitality that isn't theirs, so they require truly necessary time alone. This is the ideal opportunity for them to return, adjust, and separate themselves from all antagonism that isn't theirs.

An Empath can likewise show up as grumpy. Empaths now and again appear to have significant emotional episodes, and this is occasionally added to the majority of the staggering musings and sentiments assaulting them once a day. Not exclusively are they barraged with these energies, yet now they have to unmistakably deal with and make sense of all that stuff coming in their direction.

They are sincerely touchy to viciousness, savagery, or any kind of disaster. Most Empaths quit viewing the TV and perusing the papers sooner or later in their lives, as this as well can be overpowering for an empath.

Outright knowing is likewise a typical Empath characteristic. Empaths now and again know things that they are sure they were never instructed or told. This knowing is altogether different than instinct or a premonition.

Being in open spots is regularly overpowering or excruciating to an empath. Again such a significant number of individuals' feelings are in open places that can be grabbed when not in any case attempting to. This is a crazy ride most Empaths will maintain a strategic distance from no matter what.

An Empath can 'feel' genuineness and honesty. They can tell if somebody is being straightforward or not, which is very agitating and the time agonizing in your life. It's particularly disrupting when they are managing friends and family.

Feeling the physical manifestations and agonies of another. Numerous Empaths will end up building up a sickness that another person has that has nothing to do with them. This is compassion at its best.

These are only a couple of the characteristics of an Empath. Once more, being an Empath can be either viewed as a curse or a blessing relying upon the instruments you use to secure yourself. There are numerous ways for Empaths to protect themselves: staying away from enormous get-togethers or open places no matter what is one way. Be that as it may, there are times when you just can't evade these things. There are many useful approaches to secure yourself as an empath. This is what I like to keep in what I call 'My Bag of Tricks': I use Crystals, Meditation, and The White Light of Protection.

Crystals

Rose Quartz is an awesome gem for an Empath due to the fact that its recuperating properties advance genuine love and solace. This is particularly useful for an individual that might not hold exactly the cherishing energies of something, somebody, or even themselves.

Dark Tourmaline or Hematite is additionally incredible precious stones for an Empath to enable them to remain grounded. These stones will likewise retain any negative energy.

Malachite is another gem that will help assimilate any negative emotions you might have, regardless of whether they are your very own or not!

Labradorite is a precious stone that will really help shield your quality from retaining any issues that are being imparted to you.

Citrine is a yellow gem to help light up your state of mind. Another Citrine recuperating property is that it can likewise help assimilate awful vitality from your condition.

Amethyst. In addition to the fact that it is lovely, it will reinforce your instinct. Elevated instinct is brilliant for everybody, except particularly for Empaths, to help them genuinely realize that the emotions they might have are theirs or not.

To wrap things up is **Rainbow Fluorite**. Rainbow Fluorite might just be, as I would see it, the Mother of all precious stones for an Empath as it helps all degrees of being! This is a multi-hued gem that can enable you to remain grounded to the earth, help clear and equalize all Chakras, just as to enable you to remain sensitive to higher measurements.

Meditation

Contemplation has been utilized for a huge number of years as an approach to achieve a degree of mindfulness that is past the constraints of the consistently thinking personality. Simply, it's the act of uniting the psyche, body, and soul!

Most don't understand that our bodies were intended to act naturally, redressing to keep up positive wellbeing by basically keeping psyche, body, and soul in parity. Envision that it is so natural to be out of equalization when the vitality of others penetrates your body once a day. It's epic!

At the point when you're out of equalization, your life-power vitality doesn't stream a remarkable way it should. Being out of parity appears in life as a throbbing painfulness. Also, when you're out of parity for quite some time, your body starts to make sickness and illness.

Alone time and contemplation is a superb path for an empath to keep themselves adjusted, solid, and complete. This is simply the act of cherishing that most Empaths set at the back of the line, if they even put it in the line of significance by any stretch of the imagination!

White Light of Protection

When you just can't abstain from accomplishing things that don't top my 'wow meter, for example, going into huge groups, you ought to more often than make an effort not to ensure myself and my vitality with 'White Light'. Numerous individuals do it in different ways, and there's actually no set-in-stone manner to do it, in light of the fact that it's really about the intensity of aim.

Take a couple of minutes to yourself and sit in a tranquil spot before you do anything. Close your eyes and take a couple of full breaths. On each in-breath, imagine the white light of assurance coming into your body through your crown and filling your general existence. Proceed with taking in the white light and when your whole body is loaded up with light, envision that light currently sparkling splendidly and developing so enormous that it presently sparkles outside of you, encompassing your whole body. Sit breathing profoundly for a couple of minutes and feel the light that encompasses you. Presently grin and have a touch of appreciation since you've quite recently rehearsed self-esteem by putting yourself first. What's more, you've quite recently finished shielded yourself from all undesirable and negative energies around you!

The Anxious Empath: Anxiety and Other People's Feelings

Empaths are frequently on edge. Compassion is portrayed as the capacity to comprehend and share the sentiments of another. All people can identify snapshots of catastrophe, regardless of whether they have not encountered a comparable circumstance. In any case, sympathy is an intrinsic quality that is all the more intensely created in specific individuals from the populace (Intense Anxiety And The Highly Sensitive Person). Empaths are people who are unknowingly influenced by other individuals' mindsets, wants musings, and energies. They can actually have the feelings of others in their bodies and endeavor to convey these feelings on their shoulders while never being inquired. It's therefore, that there are frequently on edge empaths.

The Trouble with Being an Anxious Empath

It sounds great in principle; empaths are minding, comprehension, and extraordinary audience members. Be that as it may, they are frequently centered outward around others' emotions, as opposed to on themselves. As an empath, you may battle to grasp enduring on the planet and dream about fixing the majority of the world's issues.

A huge serious assignment, isn't that so?

Being this on top of others appears to be a blessing, yet empaths are burdened with the weight of their own feelings just as that of people around them. They feel a draw towards fixing, intruding, and enthusiastic comprehension, a call that regularly can't be disregarded.

The Empath's Anxiety

Empaths are experimentally demonstrated to be progressively defenseless to nervousness, social uneasiness, and sorrow. An investigation distributed in the Journal of Psychiatry shows that:

People with social fear (SP) show affectability and mindfulness to other individuals' perspectives.

Implying that people who experience the ill effects of social tension may likewise be amazingly compassionate and vulnerable to the sentiments of others. This examination infers that:

... socially restless people may exhibit an extraordinary social-intellectual capacities profile with raised psychological sympathy inclinations and high exactness in emotional, mental state attributions.

This touchiness to feelings likewise causes empaths to turn out to be sick and experience the ill effects of pressure, experience burnout in the working environment, and experience the ill effects of physical torment more frequently than others (Are You Too Sensitive? Attempt These Tips).

How an Empath can Manage Anxiety and Empathy

1. Know Your Emotional Limits

Empaths are natural healers, and individuals are frequently attracted to them hence. This makes defining practical limits so significant. Gain proficiency with the breaking points of your capacities; you can't convey the world on your shoulders, and that is alright.

2. Perceive New Feelings

Observe the manner in which various individuals make you feel - this is significant. Is it true that you are apprehensive? Do you feel profound trouble? Figuring out how the sentiments of others show in your body will enable you to all the more likely deal with the huge number of feelings you may understanding around different people (The Importance of Emotional Regulation in PTSD Recovery).

3. Discover an Outlet

Empaths typically drive their sentiments aside, trying to help other people. Feelings consistently discover an exit plan in the body. Make it a point to build up a daily practice or propensity that you appreciate and one that encourages you to communicate. You can't pour from a vacant cup (Why Self-Care is Important for Your Physical and Mental Health).

4. Use Grounding Techniques

At whatever point feelings become excessively solid, check out the space to ground yourself. Discover an article, not an individual, to study and concentrate on. Monitoring its highlights can ground you at the time and bring your outside of the exceptional sentiments occurring in your body (Top 21 Anxiety Grounding Techniques).

Make Empathy A Gift By Managing Anxiety

Being an incredibly compassionate individual, particularly an on edge empath, can frequently feel like a weight. You may feel as though your nerves are actually ablaze when you stroll into new circumstances or when you watch the news. Your uneasiness may even fool you into deduction you need to fix the whole world (Anxiety Affects Our Perspective). This can cause indications like weakness and stomach-related issues or the numerous different side effects empaths face.

Additionally, there might be a hereditary part, as social uneasiness might be to some degree bound to happen when you have a first-degree relative (parent, kin, or kid) who likewise has social tension.

There are mental and ecological explanations behind social tension too. Past encounters in which you were mortified or prodded could have added to your extraordinary nervousness, or you may have watched another person being embarrassed thusly. Having over-defensive guardians who didn't enable you to learn legitimate social aptitudes could be an explanation also.

The physical indications include:

- blushing
- profuse perspiring
- trembling
- nausea or stomach trouble
- rapid heartbeat
- shortness of breath
- dizziness or dizziness
- headache
- feelings of separation or loss of control

The passionate side effects include:

- anxiety in social settings
- high levels of dread of being judged or that others will see your nervousness
- nervousness and stress over being humiliated or embarrassed
- rumination about your nervousness
- fear of being the focal point of consideration
- avoidance of getting things done or being with individuals because of nervousness
- using medications or liquor to oversee social uneasiness
- as an empath, you feel overpowered and passionate in certain social settings

Individuals with social uneasiness will, in general, mastermind their lives around their tension. They attempt to stay away from individuals and circumstances that trigger their feelings of trepidation or outrageous feelings. In any case, when they do go to get-togethers, they stress too much before the occasion, and they invest a great deal of energy a while later rationally checking on apparent negative social circumstances and how they accept others assessed them.

Empaths likewise need to invest energy de-compacting from the majority of the serious feelings they involvement with specific gatherings of individuals.

Shockingly, social uneasiness regularly goes connected at the hip with liquor misuse, despondency, and different issue. So it's basic to your wellbeing and enthusiastic prosperity to make a move to treat the turmoil and figure out how to deal with the side effects.

Step-by-step instructions to Overcome Social Anxiety (as an empath or non-empath)

As indicated by the Social Anxiety Institute, "enormous scale, long-go (i.e., longitudinal) thinks about over the past decade have reliably demonstrated Cognitive Behavioral Therapy (CBT) to be the main treatment that can be constantly depended upon to help individuals conquer clinical uneasiness issue." CBT has been the main kind of treatment for all time to lighten nervousness issues.

CBT essentially includes figuring out how to change the manner in which you consider your social nervousness (the subjective part), just as adapting new practices in the circumstances that trigger your tension (the conducting part).

The most significant part of CBT for social nervousness is to enable you to approach social circumstances and remain with them so you, in the long run, discover that nothing downright awful will transpire. After some time, your nervousness will die down.

If you are an empath and profoundly touchy, you may need to structure CBT in a manner that shows you how to choose constructive individuals and situations that don't flood your sentiments or overpower you.

Psychological, social treatment ought to be directed with an authorized guide prepared in CBT. Your advisor will work with you in an individual or gathering setting and will probably be allocated schoolwork to rehearse between sessions. If you trust you are exceptionally delicate, let your specialist know with the goal that the individual can tailor your treatment to your particular responses and convictions.

One of the primary objectives of CBT is to enable you to distinguish the unreasonable convictions and consider yourself and your social tension, and after that, supplant those convictions with a progressively reasonable point of view. A portion of the convictions and sentiments you may take a shot at would include:

- misperceptions about your capacities and self-esteem
- guilt, shame, or displeasure regarding past circumstances
- having an absence of emphasis and certainty
- releasing compulsiveness and being progressively sensible about yourself
- dealing with shirking and hesitation identified with social nervousness
- feelings that you are odd, excessively touchy, or excessively enthusiastic

As you change your center convictions about yourself, the manner in which others see you, and your sentiments about social nervousness, you'll start to see an improvement in your uneasiness side effects.

Negative Thought Patterns

One of the most incapacitating issues you experience with social nervousness is the propensity to have to circle negative reasoning examples. You've built up these programmed perspectives after some time, yet they aren't lined up with the real world, and they increment your uneasiness and decrease your capacity to adapt.

You likely locate these negative musings happen the minute you consider an uneasiness inciting circumstance. In case you're an empath, you may expect that each social circumstance will overpower and agonizing.

After some time, your mind has progressed toward becoming wired through redundancy to have negative, restless contemplations. It should be re-prepared to think in another manner through training and reiteration, consistently for a while.

A successful method for killing negative convictions is by testing them. Ask yourself these inquiries to enable you to diffuse the intensity of your convictions:

- How are your convictions causing you to carry on?
- Would you judge another person who felt like you do similarly?
- Are you being reasonable for yourself?

- Are you going in for character death rather than adhering to what occurred on one specific event?
- Are you overlooking that everybody commits errors and feels socially awkward on occasion?
- Are you disregarding your qualities and concentrating on your shortcomings?
- Are you falling into a one-sided example of reasoning?
- Are you reaching determinations dependent on your adolescence or pre-adult encounters?
- Are you making a decision about yourself as you have once been judged?

There are commonly a larger number of points of view to a circumstance than your recognitions and convictions uncover. By analyzing your convictions and testing them, you'll start to see elective perspectives or even how your discernments may be totally false.

As you work on discovering yourself in negative reasoning examples and you kill those contemplations, your memory procedures will be affected, and the neural pathways in your cerebrum will change. You'll start to think, act and feel in an unexpected way — however, this is certainly not a one-and-done arrangement. It will take tirelessness, practice, and tolerance for advancement to be made.

Changing Your Behaviors

Another important piece of treating social nervousness through CBT is changing your programmed practices. Regularly individuals with social tension create "security practices" to keep themselves at arm's good ways from awkward circumstances or to enable them to adapt to physical responses to their uneasiness.

For instance, they may evade certain circumstances, hang out on the fringe of a get-together, over-practice things to state at a gathering, or keep their knees bolted together, so others won't see them trembling. Empaths may create wellbeing practices to enable them to maintain a strategic distance from emotional overstimulation and pessimism. Yet, even empaths can figure out how to adjust to specific circumstances and stretch themselves so as to prevail at work and in social settings.

Chapter Nine

Techniques for Empath and Sensitive People

You can't change the way that you are an empath. This is how you are made at the soul level, and you can't change this otherworldly blessing. A few people talk about turning on and off being an empath; this is somewhat deceptive in light of the fact that it is beyond the realm of imagination to expect to kill this capacity on and freely. What you can do is turned out to be mindful. Being an empath is the sort of person you are, and you are here to figure out how to utilize your empathic blessing as an amazing asset for sign and self-change.

How about we plunge into my most helpful otherworldly clearing methods that I use myself as an empath and that I prescribe to my customers:

1. Cutting The Cords

This is a significant undertaking that empaths need to turn out to be dexterous at. Since you are so great at connections and individuals cherish you, they likewise remove your vitality from you because your vitality feels so great, recuperating and adoring. This happens due to the fact that you permitted it without knowing.

At various times associations or etheric ropes with relatives, companions, and sweethearts can, in any case, be available even after the relationship is finished. It's a great opportunity to cut the strings!

To cut lines, just think about the individual with which you have had a relationship and imagine the string being cut. Favor the individual and state the accompanying: "I presently discharge you in affection and light."

There are further developed systems on the best way to cut ropes; however, this basic technique is as compelling. My conclusion is that the more we need to confound things, the more things get convoluted. It's up to you! My recommendation is to make it straightforward and make it simple. Be that as it may, do it and do it as frequently as you feel the need.

For instance, before nodding off every night, ask yourself: "Do I have any connections or lines with anybody that I met today?" If you discover something, discharge it and favor it.

Return a couple of days after the fact to ensure that the rope has been discharged. If you don't know or feel that the string is still there, get proficient assistance. I regularly discover ropes associated with one of the chakras or appended to the vitality field.

2. Clearing Your Aura from Negative Thought-Forms

Your psychological body is always communicating with the psychological assortment of others, so you get adverse musings from other individuals.

You likewise make your own considerations, and huge numbers of them may not be in arrangement with your most noteworthy great. Know about the accompanying kind of considerations:

- Negative
- Redundant
- Repetitive

- Automatic

If you need to find out about your reasoning, for example, convey a journal with you and record every one of the musings that you have inside a 24-hour time span. You will be shocked by the fact that it is so difficult to monitor your musings!

At the point when your musings are certain, you adjust to positive vibrations, and you make recuperating, equalization and concordance. When they are negative, they make obstructions and blockages.

Negative idea structures can be sustained for a considerable length of time, particularly when associated with a horrendous encounter.

These negative idea structures are made by negative understanding and desires. The more vitality you give them, the more vitality they obtain and the more grounded their impact on your condition of equalization.

They can be founded on supposition and desires for other individuals. In any case, they can stall out in your brain and happen again and again undetected until you begin to focus and effectively choose to watch your idea patterns.

Contemplations that are made out of dread, sadness, dread, fault, and outrage stay appended to your vitality field and cause you to vibrate increasingly more in arrangement with these sorts of energies. After some time, they cause you to draw in these very encounters throughout your life.

These idea structures vibrate inside you so that they catalyze a fell response at all the degrees of your vitality bodies: profound, mental, enthusiastic, and physical. They cause you to pull in individuals, circumstances, and experiences that are in vibrational arrangement with them. It resembles a greeting for low energies to connect to your vitality field.

To clear these examples, take a gander at your life and check whether you are pulling in circumstances you don't care for. If you do, you are, by one way or another vibrating in arrangement with them without your conscious mindfulness.

Your undertaking is to check in with your vitality field a few times during the day, particularly if you feel worn out and discouraged, to check whether you have got or made any negative idea structure and intentionally let it go.

3. Adjusting Your Chakras

Chakra adjusting for empaths is an absolute necessity, and it's a day-by-day practice. Two times per day, morning and nighttime, you have to take a couple of minutes to wash down your chakras.

4. Make A Sacred Space

This is so significant for everybody, except particularly on the off chance that you are an empath. A consecrated space can be any area in your home where you can be independent of anyone else and see a spot as completely self-communicated.

This could be your craft room, your contemplation room, or just your office. This spot must be yours and yours alone. Try not to impart this space to other people (indeed, you children and pets can come in and out!). It doesn't need to be inside; it very well may be outside.

Be inventive with this; however, locate an uncommon spot for you to go at any rate once every day. If it is outlandish for you to make a genuine space, make one up in your psyche and go there. You will be astounded at what you can make in your psyche.

A few people wind up in the wide-open, others along the coastline, a desert island, a recuperating sanctuary; others see themselves on different planets, out in space, or a spaceship made totally of light vitality.

5. Smearing Yourself And Your Environment

I cherish this part, and it is an absolute necessity, particularly when you feel down, pitiful, or restless. Smearing your vitality field and the earth truly transmutes negative energies from your vitality field.

Do this regularly, particularly if you have been in circumstances that made you feel out of synchrony with your passionate, mental and physical body. Utilize white sage. Additionally, remember to smirch your home normally to keep the vitality of your living space crisp and clean.

6. Interface With Nature

For anyone who feels overpowered by passionate pressure and mental anguish, nature gives the best type of vitality recuperating accessible. It is my conviction that empaths are here right now to help the vigorous frequencies important to clean the planet.

Most negative considerations and negative feelings are conveyed by people. In this way, if you are an empath, proceed to invest energy in nature alone in any event once every day to energize, you will enable nature to purge you. Contacting a tree can enable you to ground and wipe out undesirable energies from your body.

Associating with creatures, blossoms, floods of water, and normal scenes is the most relieving vitality recuperating treatment you can get. What's more, it's free!

Sit on the ground with your back against the storage compartment of a tree or stroll around with uncovered feet to drawn positive energies from the earth. This strategy is called establishing or earthling, and it will make you feel great.

7. Utilize Protective Stones

I don't accept that we should always be worried about security since I accept that we are the main expert in our life. Accepting that we need steady assurance can draw in the negative contemplations of debilitation, dread, and victimhood.

To ensure your vitality field, you should know about your vitality.

I do accept that empaths need to discover approaches to keep themselves grounded and purified constantly. This is, as I would like to think, the best type of insurance.

After the Heart-Wall clearing, it's essential to put a shield of insurance around the heart to keep the heart totally protected and ensured negative structure energies and consistently in arrangement with positive energies. When you have cleared your Heart-Wall and put a shield of insurance, you should simply enact your shield.

When I work with individuals, I instruct essentially vitality methods that they can use to ensure their auric field, yet I don't advance the requirement for insurance as much as the requirement for vitality mindfulness.

When we are intentionally mindful of our vitality, we can't fall casualties of others except if we permit it. Your energies should always be moving in doing what we are here to do as empaths: process, transmute and intensify vitality. If you are not doing this throughout the day, you will feel dormant vitality. Frequently time this is the motivation behind why you fall back into the negative part of your blessing and feel the requirement for insurance.

In this way, working with gems and stones encourages you to remain focused and mindful of what's happening in your life. This isn't anything but difficult to do when you are out there, in reality, making your background. Be that as it may, you need not free core interest. Be over your vitality!

8. Use Journaling, Art, and Drawing

Empaths will, in general, be extremely imaginative and love communicating their own ability when they feel incredible. When they don't feel extraordinary, they will, in general, oppose their imaginative capacities since craftsmanship necessitates that they work with their sentiments, and this can regularly cause torment.

I welcome you to think about utilizing workmanship as a type of recuperating and enthusiastic discharge to help you when you feel stuck and out of equalization.

9. Cry As A Form Of Emotional Release

Empaths have a very refined enthusiastic body, and they have to cry when they want to do as such. Crying has such a large number of mending benefits. The vibration of crying fills in as a purging system for your emanation. Kids do this constantly.

Doing Yoga, Tai Chi, or different types of vitality development can be exceptionally valuable to help discharge pressure, let go of undesirable negative energies, purge the emanation and realign the body and chakra framework.

Likewise, doing vitality work is the most ideal approach to keep your air washed down and incongruity with your spirit's way.

10. Ocean Salt Baths

Ocean salt has stunning purifying capacities. Ocean salt coaxes vitality out. Having a hot shower containing ocean salt when you feel vigorously overpowered can truly have a tremendous effect on how you feel. You can utilize ordinary ocean salt, Himalayan salt, Epsom salt, or others.

You can likewise include a couple of drops of fundamental oil in the water. If you have sensitivities, make a point to test them first. The best basic oils to use for purifying the emanation are rosemary, citronella, and eucalyptus.

Ways to Heal Empath

1. It isn't Necessary to Take Responsibility for Other People's Hurt

If you are an empath, you are finely tuned to the agony of other individuals, having a tendency to disguise it as your own. Keep in mind that there is just so a lot you can truly do to support other individuals. Obviously, you can attempt to support them or guide them as much as you see fit, yet toward the day's end, the individual encountering the first agony must be happy to help themselves for any evident recuperating to happen. Regularly our minding natures daze us to the way that numerous individuals don't need or aren't set up to be fixed because they are content in the security of their hopelessness.

2. Go into Your Pain Rather Than Trying to Escape from It

It sounds outlandish, doesn't it, "going into your torment"! However, it's a significant advance to discharging the repressed vitality within you. When we are engrossed with evading, stifling, and keeping away from our torment, we sustain the cycle of our torment. As opposed to yielding to the impulse to run – stop – stay composed. Plunk down and let yourself feel the exhaustion, the perplexity, the outrage, the hurt. Just once you face the reality of the torment you feel, can you at that point progress to the following phase of releasing the torment.

3. Understand That as an Empath, You Are Not Immune to Projecting Your Feelings onto Others

Let's face it here. Some portion of the intrigue of recognizing as an empath is that it once in a while gives an entryway of departure to us, a chance to stick the fault on others. Indeed, you may absorb the feelings of others like a wipe, yet that doesn't imply that you are excluded from making and profoundly encountering your own feelings. It is very simple to depict ourselves as exploited people throughout everyday life and a lot harder to assume liability for our own bliss. A key acknowledgment on the way of recuperating as an empath is to figure out how to recognize what WE are feeling from what OTHERS are feeling. Also, there isn't constantly a well put together qualification. Regularly you will find that you are feeling about 45% of the feelings, and others are feeling about 55% of the feelings, or you may feel 20% and others 80%, and the other way around.

4. Confidence Plays a Big Role in Your Ability to Deal with Your Empathic Traits

Empaths with low confidence will endure significantly more than those with solid and adjusted confidence. Self-evident? Maybe. However, not generally. Being an empath can be befuddling, and it tends to be extremely simple to accuse the misery and uselessness we feel on the barrage of improvements we experience each day. It understands that the more love, regard, and trust you create in yourself, the less you endure and that contemplations, for example, "I'm reviled," "I'm so peculiar and not quite the same as everyone," "I abhor being an empath, etc. are all regularly results of low confidence.

5. Being an Empath Is Not the Same as Having Empathy

This was hard for me to learn. "I should have loads of compassion in case I'm an empath, right?" was the supposition I used to make. In any case, I wasn't right. On account of my genuinely hindered childhood, I was a touchy youngster … but I came up short on a great deal of compassion for other individuals. Sympathy isn't empathy; it isn't feeling frustrated about individuals and needs to support them. No. Compassion is the capacity to look past the shallow façade of what an individual says and does, comprehend their circumstance, and comprehend their practices, convictions, emotions, and qualities. Having compassion is tied in with getting individuals, and in the expressions of sympathy progressive Roman Krznaric, it is tied in with taking a "creative jump into the shoes of another." Empathy is especially a scholarly and enthusiastic experience consolidated, though being an empath is a sensation, physical and passionate experience. Truly, you may have the option to share the sentiments of another, yet that doesn't really imply that you comprehend the other individual on a level further than feelings. Understanding that being an empath doesn't rise to sympathy helped me to develop colossally as an individual.

6. Protecting Is Not a Useful Technique

As a brief strategy, protecting can be useful, yet it's anything but a long-haul arrangement. I've expounded on protecting yourself previously and how it utilizes the language of victimhood, which is counterproductive to turning into an amended empath. Protecting is basically about opposing either individual's vitality, and opposition just serves to proceed with the cycles of dread and agony inside. As opposed to battling, open yourself. Enable yourself to encounter the feelings, yet in addition, let them go by not receiving them as yours. This requires significant investment and practice. However, non-connection is a vastly improved long-haul arrangement.

7. Purge and Body-Mindfulness

As an empath, it is essential to the point that you join some steady type of purification into your regular everyday practice to free yourself of the stuffy vitality you may harbor. Favored types of purge among empaths incorporate journaling/composing, reflection, strolling, and running. Different types of purification incorporate singing, moving, shouting (secretly), snickering, and crying. It is additionally amazingly gainful as an empath to show yourself how to connect with your body – I call this "body-care" or "substantial care." Basically, figuring out how to be in contact with your body is a great method for tying down and establishing yourself right now instead of becoming mixed up in the surge of feelings and impressions that come in your direction. Body-care is additionally a decent method for figuring out how to tune in to your needs, just as sustaining and dealing with yourself. I expounded more on the most proficient method to rehearse this type of care here.

How to Cope with Stress When You're Highly Sensitive

If you are thinking about whether you are an exceptionally touchy individual, it is very conceivable that you really are. This reality may influence your association with worry in your life. Individuals who are considered "exceptionally delicate individuals" will, in general, feel things more profoundly than others, identify life's nuances all the more effectively, and be progressively receptive to upgrades both inner and outer. They are individuals who might be progressively irritated by a bothersome shirt or a rough companion. They are additionally individuals who will see when somebody needs an embrace or recognize when something terrible is going to occur and change course.

Lamentably, this elevated affectability and mindfulness can convert into watchfulness, rumination, and additional worry now and again. Here is how to adapt to the extra and one-of-a-kind worry of being a profoundly touchy individual, regardless of whether the delicate individual is you or somebody you care about.

Set up Boundaries

When we discuss "limits," we mean limits in your connections, however we mean it in different ways too. This implies ending up progressively open to telling individuals where you stand and what you need—great limit-setting methods. However, we likewise mean things like making some additional squirm room in your calendar so you don't feel pushed when things unavoidably turn out badly, heap on, or require an additional reaction from you.

Practice Mindfulness and Meditation

These practices are firmly identified with defining limits. That is because this includes making a border around your encounters throughout everyday life and your considerations and emotions about them through the acts of reflection and care.

When you practice contemplation, you figure out how to step back and watch your musings and sentiments, and even your physical responses as discrete from your life and your "self." With training, a couple of significant things occur. You figure out how to quiet your body all the more rapidly, switching your pressure reaction and coming back to a position of tranquility. You additionally figure out how to segregate from things genuinely more effectively so if things feel overpowering, you don't get cleared away in the surge of feeling as effectively. It causes you to remain grounded; it can likewise assist you with building strength to stretch. The majority of this should attempt for anybody, yet this is especially valid for the exceptionally touchy individual.

"Relaxing Zones" for Yourself

This can mean having your house be mitigating and generally free of contention. This should be possible by adding a couple of components known to calm pressure, for example, alleviating music and fragrance-based treatment and having "downtime" there all the time.

This can likewise imply that you keep your cozy connections as strife-free as would be prudent. This can be practiced by learning compromise systems and emphatics, the two of which can give you the tools you need to work through troubles that may emerge among you and your friends and family.

At last, it likewise implies that you can pick individuals throughout your life to be a piece of your inward hover after they have substantiated themselves deserving of it, and you can put separation among yourself and the individuals who channel you, disappoint you, or downgrade you. When you have a steady hover of individuals who will tune in and care when you have an issue to manage in your life, it tends to be considered all the more calming to you on the off chance that you are delicate; touchy individuals need to feel comprehended and bolstered somewhat more than others, and they are superb in their ability to offer this back also. Be that as it may, it is essential to spare your strength for the individuals who will return it, at any rate to some degree, as opposed to the individuals who will deplete you and desert you or motivate self-question.

Practice Self-Care

As an exceptionally delicate individual, you are most likely progressively powerless to the attacks of lack of sleep, poor nourishment, and burnout. This implies you should make certain to get enough rest around evening time (or supplement with snoozes when essential), eat well dinners, and deal with your body, brain, and soul in the manners in which you can. This will leave you increasingly ready to deal with whatever comes your direction.

Know Your Triggers

Exceptionally touchy individuals all have their one-of-a-kind difficulties. It recognizes what stresses you the most so you can dodge these things throughout your life. Focus on how you feel during the day, and even keep up a pressure diary if necessary. Be proactive in including strength-building rehearses, just as wiping out stressors at whatever point conceivable.

You will be unable to change the way that you are delicate, yet you can completely change your way of life and propensities with the goal that you're less influenced by those stressors you can't control. Sooner or later, this will turn out to be natural, and you will feel stronger toward worry as a rule. At that point, you can just appreciate the advantages that accompany being delicate.

Strategies to Help Highly Sensitive Person

As indicated by Dr. Aron, roughly 15-20% of the populace is exceptionally touchy; truth be told, it is likely an attribute you acquired. HSP's take in tactile data in an extremely simple and developed manner. Commotions, scents, and visual subtleties that non-HSP's would probably disregard are effectively seen and prepared by HSP's. While I would characterize myself as a moderate HSP, there are sure triggers I presently perceive that enhance my affectability, and the absence of rest is one of them. Having kept awake until late to play cards the prior night figured into my response at the gathering the following day. Here are eight endurance techniques for HSP's:

- Get sufficient rest. Your body needs sufficient recuperation time from the incitement. Seven to eight hours is basic.
- Have an out. If you are investing energy with a gathering of individuals who have numerous exercises arranged, especially in a short measure of time, have a leave procedure set up if you get over-animated.
- Schedule day-by-day vacation. HSP's need time to loosen up and thoroughly consider the day.
- Limit or evade caffeine. For non-HSP's, caffeine may give a little lift, yet for HSP's, caffeine is the rocket fuel that can really cause over-arousal and block execution.
- Reframe the circumstance. Locate an elective method to see the occasion.
- Go outside. Numerous HSP's discover nature alleviating. I cherish investing energy in lakes and waterways.
- Take regular breaks. Your body needs time to process, and after that, recuperate from the incitement.
- Set limits. As an HSP, it's anything but difficult to stall out dealing with other individuals' wrecks and engage in circumstances that aren't generally your concern. Defining limits will help control your characteristic propensity to do this.

Improving Your Psychic Ability

Confidence has it that all individuals have psychic capacities in their own particular manners. How they grow, direct and train their capacities is the thing that decides how well they prevail in the aptitude. There is constantly a possibility to extend one's capacity in each proportion of life.

Growing psychic capacities and use

Psychic capacities are augmentations of forces that are typical to us. A genuine model is a perceptiveness that stretches out the capacity to see, while clairaudience stretches out the capacity to hear things. Every psychic capacity is upgraded dreams of things that are typical and normal for every single person.

In any case, one must have an uplifting disposition, unwind and trust in progress. Instinctive capacities empower individuals to contact various types of data at times simultaneously. This internal power is a well of learning dwelling inside our more profound focal being. Specialists have demonstrated that positive reasoning and energy in life increment clairvoyant capacities consequently. When one is progressively energetic, they will undoubtedly have more capacities that may make them think bigger. Then again, wariness obstructs the psychic improvement capacity.

Keeping up an inspirational outlook expects one to peruse moving and elevating writing. Perusing a couple of pages a day toward the beginning of the prior day setting out on work or starting in the day's exercises empowers one to begin the correct balance and keep up objectivity during the day. Utilizing attesting explanations is useful as well. Posting positive notes around the home, place them on the ice chest on the mirror, and others, they must be in a position where they are effectively readable.

Improving psychic capacities through unwinding

The capacity to unwind altogether and the awareness of the brain is the start of improving one's psychic capacities. Unwinding helps in modifying one's perspective and empowers the mind to accelerate its waves. Breathing now eases back from the typical rate, and the body winds up utilizing less oxygen while additionally bringing down the metabolic rate. These outcomes in less strain, expanded cell fix, and development increasing speed where the body exploits the casual situation to dispose of poisons.

In order to unwind, sit serenely in a seat with the two feet on the floor and the legs parallel to one another with the back straight up. The head ought to adjust consequently. Shoulders and arms can hang freely with the hands-on the lap and eyes shut. While in this position, start breathing gradually, enable the guts to completely fill up with air, in this position start a breathing mood. With each exhalation, insist the arrival of every one of life's anxieties and issues.

Approaches to utilize psychic capacities

To improve psychic capacities altogether, one needs to rehearse around fifteen minutes consistently. With all gadgets like telephone, TV, and radio switched off, locate a serene spot inside the home. Clairvoyant capacities are worked with time and tolerance and rehearsing the strategies utilized in unwinding after some time. While a few people are brought into the world psychics others, need to buckle down at it and practice after some time to achieve a gainful level both to themselves and to other people.

Chapter Ten

Safety Precautions against Empath

Endurance Tips for Empaths and Highly Sensitive People

If you are an empath or profoundly delicate individual, it can appear as though your own reality is persistently attacked by the vitality and sentiments of everyone around you. This can wear you out and channel you of your own life power if you are not cautious, which is the reason it is so imperative to use the majority of the methods for dealing with stress talked about underneath.

Your giving nature and profoundly adjusted faculties are blessings to this world, yet without legitimate consideration, they risk being lost. In case you're an empath, I encourage you to keep this rundown close within reach for those occasions when the external universe is hurting your internal universe.

1. Recognize Drains and Energizers

The first and most significant thing that you, as an empath, can do is to make sense of when and how your vitality gets depleted and, comparatively, those things that help to invigorate you.

With this learning, you can attempt to maintain a strategic distance from circumstances, puts, and even individuals who sap your vitality while ensuring you invest enough energy accomplishing the things that renew your stores.

It might sound straightforward, however, stemming the stream out and boosting the stream in are fundamental components for empaths to endure yet thrive.

2. Make A Shield

There will undoubtedly be a few circumstances that you, as an exceptionally touchy individual, would prefer to keep away from, yet basically can't on account of their importance in your life. Significant work capacities, enormous family get-togethers, and other get-togethers could all include individuals and energies that you discover hard to manage.

Since they are to some degree essential, you need to figure out how to adapt to such conditions, and a vitality shield is one approach to do that.

It will require exertion and practice on your part, yet in the end, you can shape a psychological boundary that lets in what you wish to let in yet diverts anything negative away. You simply need to envision an air pocket encompassing your being – an air pocket of light is a decent method to consider it. Inside this air pocket is your reality, where you can concentrate inwards and discover your parity while everything else is outward.

When you sense your vitality being depleted by other individuals or the event, you can withdraw inside your air pocket and stop the stream. Everything comes down to the consciousness of you and what's inside you.

3. Watch Your Thoughts

If you think that it's hard to assemble yourself a shield to keep negative contemplations and sentiments from attacking your psyche, the following best thing is to oversee your brain to distinguish their source.

For instance, when you end up with speculation or irate considerations, ask yourself whether this is your outrage or something that you've ingested from another. When you have worked out whose feeling it is and where it originated from, you can start a discourse in your psyche to discover an answer.

Ask yourself what the displeasure is attempting to let you know – maybe you feel something is absent from your life right now, or perhaps you discover someone else's conduct unsatisfactory.

Experience a speedy inquiry and answer session to check whether there is something that should be possible to discharge the indignation, and afterward do it.

The recognizable proof is the key here – working out what the idea is attempting to let you know and where it originated from is a certain fire approach to either possess it or scatter it.

4. Rehash Positive Affirmations

Empaths are typically open and giving individuals, yet it is not necessarily the case that they generally stay positive. Since you feel what's around you, you can experience the ill effects of pity and melancholy that aren't yours. To stay positive, it tends to be useful to have a determination of positive insistences close by to drive away from the pessimism and swim back to the light.

5. Establishing

You may find that you have a more grounded association with the Earth than the vast majority, and you can utilize this to further your potential benefit if you know-how.

It is conceivable, with training, to take any downbeat vitality and sentiments that you might have and send them into the Earth where they are assimilated. So also, the association can send positive vibes upwards and into your center.

Everything comes down to recognizing and fortifying that bond among you and the Earth.

6. Pardon

Real pardoning is the procedure by which negative vitality that has been repressed inside is discharged and waved on its way.

Regardless of whether it is an individual or something different that happened quite a while ago, as long as you clutch the hurt, it will keep on sapping you of your life power. It is only when you isolate yourself from it that you would be able to start the mending procedure.

As a delicate soul, you likely end up getting utilized and hurt more than most – it's a side-effect of your minding and giving nature – so realizing when and how to pardon is particularly significant for you.

Also, remember to excuse yourself – both for things you may have done and for enabling yourself to be harmed by others.

7. Purge

Empaths will frequently have occupied personalities that are attempting to manage the numerous feelings that barrage them once a day. It tends to be the situation that you get so enveloped with your musings that you disregard to process and cleanse the emotions that you have; rather, they get hid away and keep on influencing you.

Purification happens when you let yourself feel the feelings at their most distinctive – crying when tragic, giggling when upbeat, and shouting when irate. These are, for the most part, articulations of feelings, however, they are a lot more as well. They become outlets for the repressed vitality, regardless of whether positive or negative.

So don't be hesitant to typify the feelings, yet incidentally, with the goal that you may process and beat them.

8. Timetable Some 'You Time'

A large number of the tips in this rundown are best polished alone, which is the reason it is basic to give yourself a lot of opportunities to do only that.

Try not to feel terrible on the off chance that you need to disapprove of other individuals; your prosperity is a high need, and your loved ones will get the absolute best out of you on the off chance that they initially enable you to be without anyone else's input.

Step-by-step instructions to dispose of Empathy Deficit Disorder

Taking out Empathy Deficit Disorder

The most ideal approach to take out sympathy shortage issues is through training and mindfulness. When the influenced individual comprehends the current issue, they can begin dealing with switching it by reminding themselves not to be insensitive with their youngsters and others. At the point when this occurs, it improves the circumstance at home and works while likewise breaking the cycle by not passing it to their kids. To begin, attempt to comprehend why it is essential to annihilate the sympathy shortage issue. Kids need good examples that they look up to, for example, their folks and instructors, to react to their emotions and recognizing them. If you have a compassion shortage issue, you can start by recognizing your kid's sentiments by saying, "You look dismal", or "You appear to be irate today". This enables the kid to feel that their emotions are a typical piece of being human. Essentially, the initial step to take is to "counterfeit it". Offer compassion towards others, get some information about their emotions, and approve of them. Breathe easy in light of the information that regardless of whether you can't feel what they're encountering, you will have the option to give truly necessary help to the next individual.

Another progression to take is by giving the adoration and solace your kid needs when the individual in question is vexed. It might feel cumbersome; however, realize that it is alright to hold and embrace your kid. These activities demonstrate to the kid that you are worried about the person in question. Do whatever it takes not to tell kids that there is no utilization that they have negative sentiments. For instance, "There's no utilization being miserable, you simply need to work more diligently" may pass on the message that their emotions are not significant enough for you to mind.

Since the compassion shortfall issue isn't as of now in any indicative manual, it is up to you all together to guarantee that the passionate wellbeing in your house is kept up. If you, as of now, notice indications of sympathy shortfall issues in a few of your youngsters, you may feel overpowered at battling this issue. Be that as it may, recall that you can find a way to make the important changes. Keep in mind that while remarks, for example, "It could be more regrettable" or "You ought to forget about it," might be good-natured and essentially meant to soothe. In any case, these comments are eventually a dismissal or forswearing of what the other individual is encountering. These remarks fundamentally mean not to trouble you with their issues or not having any desire to discuss unsavory things.

After some time, you will see that your connections are improving. Inevitably, you may even feel apprehensive or miserable when you solace people around you. This can be the initial step to feeling compassion. While you may feel awkward making these initial couple of strides, attempt to expand the length you spend taking a shot at inclination sympathy.

Step-by-step instructions to Avoid the Empathy Trap

Compassion is having its minute. The capacity to feel what someone else is feeling, from that individual's point of view, creates loads of press as a definitive positive worth and the pathway to a kinder, less rough world. Schools the nation over are instructing sympathy to kids, and heap books investigate it from each conceivable edge: how to get it, why it makes you a superior individual, how its nonattendance can breed abhorrent.

Compassion is lifted by scholars from Zen Buddhist priest Thích Nhất Hạnh to British essayist Roman Krznaric, who just propelled an online Empathy Museum where you can, for all intents and purposes, step into another person's point of view. Built-up researchers like primatologist Frans de Waal and formative specialist Daniel Siegel investigate the profound underlying foundations of compassion in creatures and its basic nature in people. Indeed, even the business world lifts up compassion as an approach to guarantee the accomplishment of organizations and their items, with configuration firm IDEO driving the charge. We are admonished to look at our empathic limit and taught how to create it in ourselves and in our youngsters.

It is ordinary and important to be fixed on another person's emotions, particularly when one is exceptionally near that individual. Actually, giving—and getting—compassion is fundamental in cozy grown-up connections. "The empathic comprehension of the experience of other individuals is as essential a blessing of man as his vision, hearing, contact, taste, and smell," watched noted psychoanalyst Heinz Kohut. The longing to be heard, known and felt profoundly never vanishes. Be that as it may, when sympathy turns into the default method for relating, mental prosperity is ruined.

Where compassion is the demonstration of inclination for somebody ("I am so sorry you are harming"), sympathy includes feeling with somebody ("I feel your mistake"). It likewise varies from sympathy, which is thinking about another's experiencing a somewhat more prominent separation and frequently incorporates a longing to help. Compassion includes sentiments as well as contemplations, and it envelops two individuals—the individual we are feeling for and our own self.

To place ourselves from another person's point of view, we should find some kind of harmony among feeling and think and among self and others. Something else, compassion, turns into a snare, and we can feel as though we're being held prisoner by the sentiments of others. The specialty of sympathy requires focusing on another's necessities without giving up one's own. It requests the psychological expertise to change attunement from others to self. What transforms sympathy into a genuine high-wire act is that its recipients discover the consideration profoundly fulfilling. That puts the onus on us to realize when to separate ourselves from another person's shoes—and how.

Perceiving and sharing another person's enthusiastic state is a complex internal encounter. It approaches mindfulness, the capacity to recognize your very own sentiments and those of others, the expertise to take another's viewpoint, the capacity to perceive feelings in others just as oneself, and the ability to manage those emotions.

Excessively empathic individuals may even lose the capacity to comprehend what they need or need. They may have a reduced capacity to settle on choices in their own wellbeing, knowledge physical and mental fatigue from avoiding their very own sentiments, and may need interior assets to give their best to key individuals throughout their life. In addition, unending sympathy makes weakness to gaslighting, in which someone else discredits your very own existence to state his or hers. For instance, when you express your displeasure to your companion about being rejected from her last few social gatherings, and she answers, "Gracious, you're simply being excessively delicate."

The individuals who consistently organize the sentiments of others over their own needs frequently experience summed up uneasiness or low-level gloom. They may portray a sentiment of void or distance or harp relentlessly on circumstances from the viewpoint of another. Be that as it may, what makes us fall into a sympathy trap—and how might we escape? Here are a few thoughts.

The underlying foundations of sympathy

Children appear on the scene arranged to be empathic. Young newborn children cry because of the trouble of others, and when they can control their bodies, they react to those out of luck, to solace or offer a Band-Aid. Children fluctuate in how much they are empathic; there is by all accounts a hereditary segment and a hormonal premise to compassion. While progesterone supports sympathy, testosterone doesn't. Be that as it may, there are no reasonable sexual orientation contrasts in empathic capacity right off the bat throughout everyday life.

Much as the limit with respect to compassion is incorporated with the sensory system, it is likewise adapted, strikingly from warm and adoring guardians reflecting sentiments back to their kids. Practically all guardians treasure the minute when a youngster suddenly offers a most loved toy to soothe misery. Incidentally, however, numerous guardians quit "seeing" their kids' kindnesses around age more than two, and empathic practices level as guardians begin to compensate progressively psychological, accomplishment arranged practices.

Afterward, guardians may end up empowering compassion once more to shape conduct or sustain a youngster's very own sympathy. Think about the grown-up telling a high school child, "I see how significant that occasion is to you—you urgently need to go—and I realize that you feel truly smothered by our choice."

Be that as it may, now and then, kids are encouraged to see things through a parent's or kin's eyes, for instance, putting aside their very own advantages to visit a debilitated relative. Numerous youngsters are routinely approached to dismiss their very own sentiments so as to "be there for other people." It might later be hard for them to build up a decent feeling of sympathy.

It is a piece of the human experience to put another person's emotions before your own now and again, however not reliably. Ineffective grown-up connections, the progression of sympathy is proportional: Partners offer power similarly and move to and fro among giving and getting. When one accomplice accomplishes a greater amount of the giving, in any case, disdain is probably going to manufacture.

Sexual orientation socialization can add to empathic unevenness. Men who have been urged to "stand up" to struggle may turn out to be excessively overwhelming or, then again, pull back notwithstanding somebody's solid sentiments, not realizing how to react without dominating or surrendering. Numerous ladies are raised to accept that sympathy, all by itself, is constantly fitting, and it turns into their default method of reacting to other people. The high respect where empathic individuals are held darkens the way that they might disregard their very own sentiments.

Circumstances of inconsistent power can likewise make irregularities between accomplices in giving or accepting compassion. Think about an outrageous condition, the Stockholm disorder, in which prisoners come to express devotion and compassion toward their captors. Upon salvage, a recently liberated individual communicates understanding for the captors' activities, now and again even the longing to stay in contact with or to serve them. Battered ladies and manhandled kids frequently structure comparable bonds with their abusers.

Unfortunately, seeing someone set apart by inconsistent power, those in the low-control position are bound to concede to the necessities of those in the powerful position. Doing so causes them to clutch the connection—at the expense of turning into the engineers of their own disappointment.

A few circumstances, such as providing care, call for a focus on another person's needs. They can strain anybody's empathic limit. It's significant for all parental figures to discover support from individuals who can offer a similar sort of help for them.

From caught to adjusted

How would you know whether you are in danger of being caught by compassion? A yes answer to any of the accompanying inquiries should raise a warning.

- Do you invest more energy pondering your accomplice's emotions than about your own?
- Do you concentrate on what the other individual is stating during a contention, to the rejection of what you need to state?
- Do you frequently get so made up for lost time in the sentiments of somebody you cherish when they are discouraged or offending that appear to turn into your own?
- After leaving a contention, would you say you are distracted by what the other individual was thinking?
- Do you invest more energy attempting to make sense of why somebody let you down than choosing whether their reasons exceeded your sentiments?

Getting control over empathy requires enthusiastic insight; its hidden aptitude is mindfulness. You need consistently to be set up to investigate and address your very own issues. Since you're not used to contemplating them, you probably won't be completely mindful of what those requirements are. At whatever point your compassion is excited, see it as a sign to turn a focus without anyone else sentiments. Delay (taking a full breath check) in with yourself: What am I feeling at this moment? What do I need now?

When you comprehend what you need, you can settle on a cognizant choice about the amount to provide for another and the amount to a demand for yourself. Obviously, it sustains associations with individuals who are aware of the requirements of others.

Making a move on your needs approaches the expertise of self-administration. When you start seeing the manners by which you become consumed by other individuals' extraordinary sentiments, particularly their negative ones, you can make some separation—even protect yourself if important.

Things Empaths Should Try To Avoid At Any Cost

Empaths are people who make humankind wonderful. They are a strong wellspring of motivation, love, getting, compassion, and, obviously, high-recurrence vibrations. They basically improve this world a spot.

In any case, empaths are individuals with amazingly solid tangible and discerning capacities. Progressed empaths can even feel what the individuals around them feel at a particular time. That is the reason they see the world with various eyes, and they reserve the privilege to do it. This world is loaded up with self-centeredness, outrage, evilness, and realism.

1. Maintain a strategic distance from obstruction and refusal.

This is a 'difficult spot' for all empaths. They can't stand obstruction and refusal. As a matter of fact, they never need to be the focal point of consideration, nor do they need consideration, yet when they cherish somebody, their feelings are solid and unadulterated. Dismissal harms them to an extreme, driving them down in discouragement. In any case, this is extraordinary guidance for empaths-avoid individuals who don't acknowledge and adore you. You can feel it-not every person has the right to place confidence in.

2. Abstain from turning into an injured individual.

Empaths are normally amassing vitality. Positive and negative. Be that as it may, the world is, for the most part, antagonistic, so they regularly find themselves undermined by idiotic and mean individuals around them. They are extremely touchy and agreeable at a similar time, yet at the same time, they are not resistible to every single negative feeling around them. Their weight is substantial, with the goal that's the reason they ought to consistently abstain from turning into a casualty of a specific clash circumstance. Numerous other individuals who don't have compassion will utilize it as a bit of leeway against empaths and hurt them.

3. Abstain from overlooking how karma functions.

This is significant. If you are an empath, you ought to always remember the vast power and the smaller scale large-scale universe association. Each activity has a response that is the standard all empaths need to pursue.

4. Abstain from depleting yourself to weariness.

Obviously, empaths as 'sensors' register and aggregate all vitality and feelings around them. This could regularly prompt a substantial weariness. Normally, empaths want to support other individuals; however, frequently, they overlook their points of confinement. Know that not every person merits help or needs assistance and 'shoulder for crying'. Empaths ought to know about their breaking points. Mental fatigue is exceptionally difficult for them.

5. Abstain from secluding yourself.

Seclusion isn't the arrangement! Numerous empaths who don't know how exceptional they are frequently detach themselves and remain in the 'shell'. They can't stand the weight of the outside world. That is typical. In any case, they have to comprehend that they have the ability to deal with their exceptional capacities. They could be THE CHANGE in their groups of friends, and that is the way they should see themselves.

Different things an empath should carefully evade.

1. Negative news.

Ok, the news. It has dramatization. It has drama. Also, it's (regularly) got cynicism. While a decent piece of individuals might be attracted by and love these things, empaths ordinarily don't. Need to eliminate the dread, frenzy, and tension in your life? Cut out the negative news.

2. Extraordinary stimulation.

A few people love alarming, dramatic films, shows, books, and music. Empaths, be that as it may, don't. That is because we can really feel the feelings and sentiments of individuals, creatures, and things onscreen. Along these lines, where a normal individual who doesn't assimilate vitality can without much of a stretch let go of a vicious scene, the empath can't.

3. Mockery.

Wry individuals are all over the place. Be that as it may, that doesn't mean you have to endure it. Albeit a few people can dismiss sharp punches and cutting deeds, the empath can not. The explanation might be established in the word mockery itself. Starting from the Greek word "sarkazein," it signifies "to tear substance." Put basically, mockery isn't interesting; it's a threatening vibe camouflaged as silliness.

4. Constant Complainers.

If there is one sort of individual for an empath to maintain a strategic distance from other than a narcissist, it's a constant grumbler. Interminable whiners, described by antagonism, learned vulnerability, and vocal self-centeredness, can take a brilliant, excellent, positive day and rapidly transform it into an enormous bad dream. At that point, there's the issue of engrossing those things into one's vitality. If the sentiments and feelings of the individuals around an empath are certain, cheerful, and quiet, the empath feels brilliant. Assuming, in any case, the words, activities, or practices of the individual around them are centered around things like displeasure, dread, fault, or reprisal, the empath feels and may assimilate this, as well. Of course, this can prompt perplexity, outrage, and upset.

5. Enormous gatherings of individuals for broadened measures of time.

Despite the fact that not all empaths are loners, something they do share practically speaking is the capacity to feel and detect vitality – and the propensity to retain it. That is the motivation behind why your empathic companion may not be enthused about following along to that Rangers game or for after-work drinks. In spite of the fact that empaths can figure out how to deal with the energies of groups fruitful, they frequently need assistance around there. Procedures like line cutting and vivacious protecting, rehearsing sound limits, and restricting time spent in profoundly invigorating conditions are basic.

6. Exceptionally basic individuals.

The individual who composed the proverb, "Sticks and stones may break my bones, yet names will never hurt me," was likely not an empath. That is because, when you are empathic, words and names can – and regularly, do – hurt. To the layman, the capacity to "shut off" their sympathy notwithstanding disdain or outrage may come simply; that, in any case, isn't the situation with an empathic person. The reality additionally remains that being around a profoundly basic, judgmental individual isn't useful for anyone. What's more, with the ongoing revelation that feelings are for sure infectious, it just bodes well for empaths to maintain a strategic distance from the cruel treatment and antagonism of profoundly basic individuals.

Chapter Eleven

Narcissists Claiming To Be Empaths

There is an extraordinary sort of Narcissist, regularly alluded to as the "Incognito Narcissist" that just freely shows up as a run-of-the-mill, commonplace obsessive Narcissist. These are the excessively touchy and discerning Narcissists. This Narcissist does a hell of a great deal of picture the executives and is normally incredibly vital in how to make themselves look idealistic, liberal, mindful, and cherishing. This sort of Narcissist knows about their capacity to be harmed and injured and realizes they have some degree of early youth injury they stroll around with. They are especially self-defensive and hole up behind their "limits", which are an intricate arrangement of guards, loops to bounce through, and prerequisites others should meet before they "trust" you and will draw near to you.

This sort of Narcissist is typically extremely brilliant and will scan for a scholarly comprehension of why they feel so hurt by the world and search for more prominent comprehension in brain science and otherworldliness as a signal of protection from responsibility for their relationship shows and general responsibility.

In the previous years, I have watched numerous Covert Narcissists guarantee to be natural or extra-tangible Empaths as an approach to clarify their inner experience of affectability and sharp, keen mindfulness, and to guarantee a feeling of profound, clairvoyant, and relational predominance over others. What's more, because these individuals may be altogether fanciful and persuaded they are in certainty Empaths, others will, in general, trust them.

I have a sneaking doubt that in strict and profound networks, numerous masters who are taking part in sexual, manipulative, or clique-like exercises with understudies are Covert Narcissists. Really, these kinds of individuals make it into a wide range of callings and jobs, and from multiple points of view, impeccable a constructive persona while utilizing it as a well-developed shield to keep their exploited people from regularly considering them completely responsible.

All in all, given this pattern, what can we as a whole do to decide whether somebody is in truth an Empath versus a Covert Narcissist? Here are 3 techniques to test whether somebody is an Empath or a Covert Narcissist.

Three Methods to Uncover The Truth

1. Set and Reset, Boundaries.

To begin, the most ideal approach to tell if somebody is, in reality, an Empath is to consciously, and tranquility define limits and perceive how they respond. Start saying "No" to them or indicating dissidence openly. This implies, can't help contradicting them, and let others realize you are doing this. An Empath, regardless of whether at first somewhat humiliated and guarded, would consider if what they said or did wasn't right or how your point of view and experience could conceivably be substantial. They would give their vitality to getting you instead of putting their vitality into altering your perspective and dealing with their picture. To be honest, on the off chance that they react with a push to constrain you to concur, attempt to threaten or humiliate you, or attempt to cause you to apologize for deviating, this is a generally excellent sign they are not an Empath.

More on defining limits: when drawing nearer to a claimed Empath impractically, see the pace at which they need to become acquainted with you, just as in which ways they need to become acquainted with you. Frequently Covert Narcissists will push for extremely fast passion and sexual closeness, despite the fact that when you're communicating, you have a slower pace. If you start saying "Yes" to things you generally state "No" to, this is likely a direct result of their master controls are setting you in the mood for losing your limits and consequently assembling assent.

If you express, you continue experiencing issues holding your limits, and regardless of them indicating care and worry for your experience, despite everything, you end up in this circumstance; this is a HUGE sign somebody is a Narcissist. Actually, another huge contrast between Narcissists and Empaths is that Narcissists of various kinds are EXTREMELY tested in postponing delight. They will arrange their lives around the same number of kinds of moment delight as they have the assets for and will even depend intensely on others bearing them significantly more noteworthy access to moment satisfaction.

Along these lines, on the off chance that you say "No" to a (Covert) Narcissist and begin to define more grounded limits, they will probably attempt to make a circumstance with earnestness, or you have less ability to state "No", or expressly attempt to persuade you to drop the limit so they can get their satisfaction as quickly as time permits. When they don't get the delight they needed alone or from you, they will get baffled and irate. An Empath, then again, would likely re-align and acknowledge that satisfaction won't occur except if your needs are respected, and they may drop the arrangement altogether, absent a lot of dissents.

2. Watch What They Do When You Get Angry and Frustrated Around Them.

An Empath will promptly think about what has gotten you baffled and irate. If they aren't as of now making themselves accessible to enable, they to will probably express something as a type of middle-of-the-road help and consolation. You will probably feel alleviated by the manners in which they react to you and particularly feel their essence with you.

Regardless of whether a Covert Narcissist copies the practices of an Empath totally, there will be a way you unobtrusively feel they don't comprehend, are absent, or couldn't care less. You will probably feel like their assistance or consolation doesn't really do much for you and may even bring about your inclination more awful, and like you may require them considerably more for alleviating and solace.

Furthermore, if the Covert Narcissist hasn't figured out how to splendidly emulate an Empath, you will see they begin to end up restless or are then activated and, by one way or another, injured by you being irate and baffled. This is regardless of whether your outrage and dissatisfaction aren't about them or your association with them. They may make you feel regretful for burdening them or for "playing the person in question" or for being "excessively delicate" while making you feel like at the same time, regardless you need them to enable you to see the light and to feel much improved.

This, in plain talk, is them demonstrating to you whether they have genuine, effectual sympathy and not simply mentally built compassion. Trust your gut, as typically we as a whole can tell if somebody is feeling maybe compassion toward us and bolstering us a content, versus really FEELING genuine sympathy with us.

3. Ask A Lot of Pointed Questions About Their Spiritual Purpose or General Purpose on The Planet

An Empath may comprehend their motivation on this planet is to help individuals and to be a piece of maybe helping other people mend, be more joyful, and more beneficial. An Empath may not be modest about expressing this reality.

A Covert Narcissist will likewise likely accept they have a unique reason for being on the planet, and may even infer a lot of Narcissistic Supply from helping individuals, and consequently discover a lot of satisfaction in a helping calling, or possibly in encircling their calling as an accommodating one.

The fundamental contrast is the point at which you ask Empath inquiries about their way to be a healer or an aide to humankind; they, for the most part, will incorporate data about their own mending way and how it had driven them to where they are. They will likewise be mindful so as to make reference to that they can't fix or recuperate, or help everybody when you notice a setting where individuals are battling and need assistance that is past their extent of mastery or capacity.

A Covert Narcissist regularly rather depicts a ruddy and misrepresented image of their past triumphs with aiding, just as in the manner in which they imagine helping individuals later on. They additionally may paint a pretty and smooth image of their past excruciating history and how they have defeated it. It might appear as though they are asserting that with their sheer will and astonishing capacity, or the one-of-a-kind cure or aptitude they experienced, helped them essentially become illuminated. Infrequently, a Covert Narcissist has an amazingly well-curated persona of an Empathic healer and will have an account that mirrors a genuine Empath's story. Be that as it may, in the wake of posing enough inquiries, you will start to see the openings in their account and begin to perceive how shallow they really are. Regularly, they will endeavor to cut you off, vanish, or make an alternate discussion, circumstance, or show to redirect your inquiries and consideration, so they can't be discovered.

Ways That Narcissists Destroy Empaths

1 - Control

The main objective of most narcissists is controlling. That is the means by which they get what they need or make you think what they need you to think. Not all narcissists have pernicious expectations; it is only a control thing for them. Presently when an empath and a narcissist run into each other, the empath is helpless to this control more than most. For a narcissist, this resembles having a great time new toy to play with.

2 - Watchmen are Down

As an empath, we are ordinarily less monitored. It is anything but a cognizant choice; it is exactly how we are. That is the thing that makes us ready to get on the enthusiastic condition of other individuals so effectively because we aren't attempting to make sense of whether we should confide in somebody before getting sincerely appended; we simply do. For a narcissist, this resembles battling against a fighter who has his hands in his pockets (expecting boxing shorts have pockets). Those controls and controlling exercises that take work for other individuals slide directly in like unblocked punches on an empath.

3 - Clash of Egos

Narcissism is extremely a result of the inner self, and generally, Empaths are not prideful individuals. Along these lines, the narcissist's inner self, in the end, overwhelms the empath. Basically, a narcissist can make an empath into a narcissist after some time. For the empath, they begin to question themselves dependent on the control of the narcissist, and they start to feel like an unfortunate casualty. The unfortunate casualty attitude is additionally a result of the sense of self, so after some time, the empath's sentiments about themselves change.

It's a crucial move in the inner self that can prompt sadness.

At last, being an empath is intense enough, all things considered. As an empath, you know this. Monitoring the individuals around us and their effects on us is the most significant thing we can do to clutch our mental stability and self-esteem.

Empaths: How to Shield Yourself Against Narcissists

It's imperative to comprehend that being otherworldly and being an empath doesn't imply that we should continue excusing an individual again and again, at any rate, not while we're involved with them.

This goes for a sentimental or some other sort of relationship, so if you distinguish just like an empath or you presume you may have empathic characteristics, the present video will enable you to figure out how to shield yourself against narcissists.

1 – Get open to executing limits

The primary thing all empaths need to engage themselves is to acknowledge that so as to have solid connections, you'll need to arrive at a point where you feel good actualizing limits.

What I see time and again is that genuinely merciful and cherishing people don't execute limits in their connections, and after that miracle, why they are being exploited. (I used to do this as well, so no judgment there).

When we enable somebody to stomp on our limits, and we don't take care of business, we are fundamentally showing them how to treat us. Inevitably, the narcissistic individual comprehends that they can do whatever they please, and there will be no results.

When we excuse a narcissist on numerous occasions, they don't begin to address themselves; they will never have a revelation and start to see your unlimited love for them. What occurs rather is that they start to consider theirs to be maltreatment as terrible, and that is the reason their maltreatment deteriorates after some time.

Numerous individuals, maybe dependent on their strict convictions, accept that they should love instead of lashing out and live by the Golden Rule; however, that doesn't have any significant bearing on narcissists and different controllers. If you are a strict individual, the Bible and different strict writings are clear about how we should deal with such individuals.

Creator Christine Louis de Canonville once composed an arrangement dependent on entries from the Bible with respect to narcissism. Since, when she was an advisor, such a significant number of her customers battled with accepting that if they didn't choose to retaliate, they weren't pardoning and thus would not be excused themselves.

It would be ideal if you comprehend, I'm making an effort not to lecture here, yet in Christine's articles, she called attention to that narcissism is tended to in the Bible. In Paul's second peaceful epistle to Timothy, Paul appeared to be worried about the character and conduct of pioneers inside the congregation, so he cautions Timothy to know about the individuals who carry on of a sacrificial mentality:

For men will be admirers of themselves, admirers of cash, blowhards, glad, blasphemers, insubordinate to guardians, unthankful, unholy, heartless, slanderers, without discretion, fierce, despisers of good, backstabbers, having a type of righteousness, however denying its capacity... and from such individuals TURN AWAY.

Perhaps you are not a strict individual. Actually, despite the fact that I especially have faith in God, I don't pursue composed religion any more drawn out because there is such a lot of strict control vitality occurring in the present society and in my own encounters, what I saw was pioneers who needed to oversee and control individuals' otherworldly data.

I've worked with too many training customers who were threatened by pioneers inside their congregation who utilized religion as a weapon. This is the thing that I mean when I state that we are not committed to help and mend everybody around us in a crazy manner. You are not an abhorrent or narrow-minded individual for executing limits in your connections. Any individual who discloses to you that you are insidious because you go to bat for yourself is attempting to utilize strict control vitality against you.

We as a whole need limits provided that we don't have them; we will keep on drawing in individuals who are manipulative and narcissistic. Empaths would have a lot simpler time throughout everyday life if they can acknowledge that limits are critical if you need to begin having solid connections and quit feeling like a flickering neon light, bringing in each narcissist inside a hundred-mile range.

If somebody wouldn't like to change, at that point, saying no and proceeding onward is generally the main solid thing you can do.

The most cherished thing we can accomplish for another individual is to consider them responsible for their activities as opposed to tidying up the phase for them without fail. Else, we're instructing them that it's alright to keep accomplishing the harmful things that they do.

2 – The narcissist is certifiably not a tormented soul who needs your uncommon sort of adoration

How do Empaths ensure themselves against narcissists?

Pretty much every Empath who's at any point been involved with a narcissist has believed that if they could simply demonstrate to the narcissist how profound their unlimited love ran, the narcissist would, at last, have a revelation where they understood that there's an exceptional and uncommon sort of adoration accessible to them, all things considered.

The adoration for an Empath unquestionably has its recuperating characteristics; however, it does nothing to change a narcissist's practices or intentions in the relationship. Narcissists are ethically bankrupt people who don't welcome the things other individuals accomplish for them.

Difficult Truths All Empaths Must Eventually Face About Narcissists

Rather, they feel totally qualified for whatever adoration and dedication are coordinated towards them. Truly, every individual the narcissist has ever been associated with gave them this unrestricted love, however tragically, narcissists think about such love and commitment as dispensable. They instinctively realize that there are heaps of injured individuals out there who are hesitant to execute limits because of a paranoid fear of losing their connections, and most narcissists are continually exploring new supply sources.

This is absolutely why when your relationship closes, you see them with another person so rapidly. As a rule, the new individual isn't so new. The narcissist has just been preparing them for quite a while.

If any of this impacts you, it would be ideal if you realize that I see that it is so hard to begin actualizing limits in your connections when you haven't done that previously. The Way of the Warrior and Empowered Empath is biting the dust to our old ways and being renewed as the best form of ourselves where we perceive our worth and the privilege to upbeat, solid connections and, in particular, the relationship we have with ourselves.

This is the thing that my Break Free Bootcamp is about. It instructs you to enable yourself and be your very own closest companion and supporter.

How Empaths can shield themselves from narcissists

In case you're feeling apprehensive, I know how you feel. I have been there myself, and there is no most exceedingly terrible inclination on the planet other than feeling like you're in an endless bad dream, yet life doesn't need to be that way.

Each passing moment is an opportunity to turn it all around, and you can begin by making your first enabling stride and asserting your free novice's mending guide (underneath), which incorporates all that you have to begin, including a ground-breaking worksheet on deciding your limits and major issues.

Like Narcissists, All Empaths Should Look Out For

Such a large number of articles out there discussing "securing" yourself from narcissists. Sadly, this language advances the debilitating thought that "other individuals are out to get you." They're definitely not. Individuals act inside the cutoff points of their cognizant limit, and some of the time, that includes harming others. The more you see yourself as an "unfortunate casualty" of narcissists/narcissism, the less able you'll be of really owning your own capacity as an empath.

A major piece of owning this individual intensity of yours is figuring out how to recognize various sorts of narcissists. The more cognizant you are of them, the more deliberately you'll have the option to carry on and settle on choices in their quality.

Principle Types

Curiously there are really few fundamental sorts of narcissists:

1 - Powerless Narcissists (VN's)

These individuals are commonly extremely delicate and will, in general, be tranquil or timid naturally. However, to camouflage their ceaseless sentiments of self-hatred and shamefulness, VN's overcompensate by putting on a pretentious veil, trying to consolidate their characters with other glorified individuals. VN's have an unshakeable need to feel extraordinary about themselves and have minimal real respect for the sentiments of others. VN's are basically spurred by dread of dismissal and relinquishment, along these lines don't have the ability to really love and think about others. Furthermore, VN's utilization of passionate control (for example, disgracing, blame stumbling, and gaslighting) to verify compassion and consideration from others. Their lives are fuelled by feelings of inadequacy which regularly come from youth abuse.

2 - Safe Narcissists (IN's)

These individuals mirror the customary picture of the narcissist: that of a profoundly fearless individual, cold and unempathetic individual. IN's, not normal for VN's, are tough and indecently look for power, wonder, acknowledgment, and delight. IN's frequently experience the ill effects of god buildings, trusting themselves to be far better than every other person – and they have a neurotic need to make that known.

The two kinds share comparative attributes, for example, utilizing others to fuel their narcissistic hallucinations, accusing and condemning, absence of compassion, unfaithfulness, and the requirement for power.

Subtypes

Both Vulnerable and Invulnerable Narcissistic character sorts can be part down into the accompanying (informal) subtypes. Know that a large number of these subtypes can cover with one another:

3 - The Amorous Narcissist

Affectionate Narcissists measure their self-esteem and gaudiness by what number of sexual victories they have added to their repertoire. This kind of individual is known for utilizing his/her fascinate to entrap others with sweet talk and endowments, yet then rapidly discarding them once they become "exhausting" and when they have met the narcissists' needs (regularly sexual or picture/status orientated). Loving Narcissists are definitive relationship cheats, "gold diggers" and heart-breakers. From the outset, they show up exceptionally appealing, charming, and obliging, however underneath, they are just out to please and satisfy their very own needs and wants.

4 - The Compensatory Narcissist

Headed to make up for past injuries, Compensatory Narcissists love making overwhelming deceptions of themselves and their accomplishments. So as to recover power and authority over their lives, this kind of narcissist, for the most part, chases out sincerely helpless individuals who will fill in as the group of spectators to their created stage acts. In actuality, this sort of narcissist is incredibly delicate to analyze and will most of the time pay special attention to negative self-coordinated signals from others. Psychological mistreatment and control is a typical technique for control utilized by this sort.

5 - The Elitist Narcissist

This type of individual effectively moves to the "top," wins, and totally overwhelms others. Elitist narcissists are persuaded that they are superior to every other person frequently because of their accomplishments or foundations (or just the way that they were brought into the world that way) and, along these lines merit uncommon treatment. Their feeling of qualification seeps into each everyday issue, from work to the family condition. Harboring a seriously expanded personality, Elitist narcissists are talented self-advertisers, braggers, and one-uppers. They have a merciless should be simply the "best" and demonstrate to be mentally predominant constantly and no matter what.

6 - The Malignant Narcissist

The conduct of harmful narcissists regularly covers that of insane people and those with standoffish character issues. Harmful narcissists frequently have no respect or enthusiasm for good versus improper conduct and don't feel regret for their activities. This subgroup is portrayed by a presumptuous and expanded feeling of self-esteem that thoroughly enjoys "outflanking" others. This sort of narcissist can regularly be found in jails, posses, and medication recovery focuses, albeit many figures out how to cross paths with the law.

How Empaths Can Protect Themselves against Narcissists

It's critical to comprehend that being profound and being an empath doesn't imply that we should continue pardoning an individual again and again, in any event, not while we're involved with them.

Basically, being otherworldly doesn't mean being a mat.

This goes for a sentimental or some other sort of relationship, so if you recognize something similar to an empath or you speculate you may have empathic characteristics, the present video will enable you to figure out how to shield yourself against narcissists.

Get open to executing limits

The principal thing all empaths need to engage themselves is to acknowledge that so as to have sound connections, you'll need to arrive at a point where you feel good actualizing limits.

What I see time after time is that genuinely humane and adoring people don't execute limits in their connections and, after that, marvel why they are being exploited. (I used to do this as well, so no judgment there).

When we enable somebody to stomp on our limits, and we don't take care of business, we are essentially showing them how to treat us. Inevitably, the narcissistic individual comprehends that they can do whatever they please, and there will be no outcomes.

When we pardon a narcissist on numerous occasions, they don't begin to address themselves; they will never have a revelation and start to see your unequivocal love for them. What occurs rather is that they start to consider their maltreatment as awful, and that is the reason their maltreatment deteriorates after some time.

Numerous individuals, maybe dependent on their strict convictions, accept that they should love instead of lashing out and live by the Golden Rule, yet that doesn't have any significant bearing on narcissists and different controllers. If you are a strict individual, the Bible and different strict writings are exceptionally clear about how we should deal with such individuals.

Chapter Twelve

How to Train Empathy

Empaths are attracted to treating others and themselves. They are normally attracted to recovery since they think they've so much inner recovery to do... before, that is, they recognize that the majority of the recovery needed is for many others whom they've intuitively sensed.

They're generally in a condition of constant exhaustion. This is a massive issue. People, together with their energies, are constantly invading an empath's energy. An empath will generally take on too much and be emptied very fast, and it is not readily cured by rest or sleep. It goes much deeper than this and can be quite exhausting.

Empaths are excellent listeners. They really care about the well-being of others also find themselves listening to the woes of individuals they do not even understand. Many men and women find empaths really simple to start up. That is when they begin dumping all types of negativity moving in their lifetime. From time to time, individuals are not even aware they do so.

In many cases, an empath with the care of the demands of others before their own, since they care a lot better. Since folks get comfortable enough about them to start up, they will generally selflessly give their ear to aid a man, even if it's to their detriment.

Alone timing is a must for the empaths. Most empaths prefer to escape from all the emotions and energy that isn't theirs, so that they need a lot needed time. This can be time for them to return to equilibrium and distance themselves from all negativity that isn't theirs.

An empath may also look moody. Empaths occasionally appear to have significant mood swings, which occasionally is contributed to everyone the overwhelming thoughts and feelings bombarding them on a daily basis. Not only are they bombarded with those energies, but they will need to definitely sort through and find out all the things coming their way.

They're emotionally sensitive to violence, cruelty, or any kind of tragedy. Many empaths stop watching the tv and reading the papers at some time in their lives, as this also can be quite overwhelming to get an empath.

Just plain understanding is also a common empath characteristic. Empaths sometimes understand things which they're positive they were not told or instructed. This understanding is quite different than instinct or a gut sense.

Being in public areas can be overwhelming or debilitating to an empath. Again many people's emotions have been in public areas, which may be picked up when not trying to. This really is a roller coaster most empaths will prevent at any cost.

An empath can 'sense' honesty and ethics. They could tell if a person is being truthful or not, that is quite unsettling and at times debilitating in your lifetime. It is especially unsettling when they're coping with loved ones.

Feeling the bodily symptoms and pains of the next. Most empaths will end up creating a disorder that somebody else has that doesn't have anything to do together. This is compassion at its best.

All these are only some of those characteristics of an empath. Again, being an empath could be considered a curse or a blessing based upon the instruments you use to protect yourself.

There are a lot of ways for empaths to safeguard themselves. Preventing large social gatherings or public areas at all costs is one way. But there are occasions once you just can't prevent these things. There are many helpful methods to safeguard yourself as an empath. Here is what I love to bear in what I call 'my bag of tricks'. I use crystals, meditation, and the white light of protection.

Crystals

Rose quartz is a wonderful crystal for the empath since its curative properties encourage unconditional love and relaxation. This is particularly great for an individual who could be holding the less loving energies of something, somebody, or perhaps themselves.

Black tourmaline or hematite will also be great crystals to get an empath to assist them in remaining grounded. These stones may also help absorb some unwanted energies.

Malachite is just another crystal that will help absorb some negative feelings you might be having if they are your personal or not!

Labradorite is a crystal that will actually help safeguard your air from absorbing any problems which are being shared with you.

Citrine is a yellowish crystal to help decorate your disposition. Another citrine healing house is it may also help absorb poor energy out of your surroundings.

Another proceed to crystal is amethyst. Not only is it beautiful, but it is going to strengthen your instinct. Heightened intuition is fantastic for everybody, but particularly for empaths to assist them really know that the feelings that they are needing are not.

Last but not least is rainbow fluorite. Rainbow fluorite may very well be, in my estimation, the mother of crystals to get an empath because it assists all levels of being! This really is a multi-purpose crystal that could enable you to stay grounded into the ground, help equilibrium and clear all chakras, and help you remain attuned to high dimensions.

All these are my private visit crystals to allow me to remain focused, grounded, secure, and tuned in. Crystals can and will help heal your life!

Meditation

Meditation has been used for centuries as a means to achieve a degree of consciousness that's beyond the constraints of the daily believing thoughts. Quite simply, it is the custom of bringing together the brain, body, and soul!

Most do not recognize that our bodies were intended to be more self-correcting to keep positive health simply by keeping your mind, body, and soul in balance. Imagine how simple it's to be out of equilibrium once the energy of the others infiltrates your body on a daily basis. It is epic!

When you're from equilibrium, your life-force energy does not flow quite how it should. Being out of balance shows up in existence as pains and aches. When you're out of equilibrium for extended, your body starts to make disease and illness.

Alone meditation and time is a fantastic way for an empath to stay balanced, healthy, and complete. This is the tradition of enjoying yourself that many empaths place at the rear of the line, should they put it in the line of significance in any way!

White light of defense

When I simply can't avoid doing things that don't peak my 'wow meter', like moving into big audiences, I usually attempt to shield myself and my electricity together with 'white light'.

A lot of people do it otherwise, and there is no wrong or right means to do it since actually, it is about the power of intention.

Require a few moments on your own and sit at a quiet place until you do anything. Close your eyes and take a few deep breaths. On every in-breath, imagine the white light of defense coming to the human body through your crown and filling your whole being. Keep on breathing from the white light and if your whole body is full of light, envision that light now shining brightly and developing so large it now glows out you, surrounding your whole body. Sit breathing deeply for a few minutes and sense the light that surrounds you. Now smile and have a little gratitude since you have only practiced self-love by placing yourself. And you have just finished shielded yourself from all negative and unwanted energies around you!

Here are a couple of attributes of empaths who have not figured out how to sift through other individuals' feelings or deal with their very own vitality:

- You always feel overpowered with feelings, and you may cry a great deal, feel pitiful, furious, or discouraged without any justifiable cause. You might be enticed to think you are insane for having arbitrary emotional episodes and episodes of unexplained weakness. If you are a lady, it resembles having PMS constantly! Intemperate sympathy can make an individual show indications like bipolar (hyper burdensome) clutter.

- You drop by the store feeling incredible, yet once you get in a group, you start feeling down, irate, miserable or overpowered. You believe you should contract something, so you choose to return home and rest.

- If you've discovered that you can't be open without getting overpowered, you may begin to carry on with the life of a loner. However, even at home, you get discouraged when you watch the news, and you cry while viewing a film. You feel terrible when a business for the Humane Society indicates creatures that need a home. You may save a greater number of creatures than you can think about.

- You feel frustrated about individuals regardless of what their identity is or what they have done. You want to stop and help anybody in your way. You can't go by a vagrant without giving him cash regardless of whether you don't have it to save.

- Many empaths are overweight. When they assimilate unpleasant feelings, it can trigger fits of anxiety, despondency just as nourishment, sex, and medication gorges. Some may indulge in adapting to passionate pressure or utilize their body weight as a shield or cushion. In Chapter 9 of Yvonne Perry's book, she tells the best way to utilize light as assurance.

- Most empaths can physically and genuinely recuperate others by drawing the agony or sickness out of the wiped-out individual and into their own bodies. For clear reasons, this isn't prescribed except if you realize how to keep from winding up sick all the while.

- From chest torments and stomach spasms to headaches and fever, you show indications without getting a real ailment. Afterward, you discover that your "disease" matched with the beginning of a companion or relative's sickness.

- No one can mislead you since you can see through their facade and recognize what they truly mean. You may even know why they lied.

- People-even outsiders open up and start volunteering their own data. You might sit in the lounge area tending to your very own concerns and hanging tight when the individual by you starts sharing a wide range of individual data. You didn't ask them to, and they never thought that you might not have any desire to catch wind of their dramatization. Individuals may feel better in the wake of talking with you, yet you end up with more terrible inclination because they have moved their passionate torment to you.

- Some empaths don't do well with close connections. Always taking on their accomplice's agony and feelings, they may effortlessly get their sentiments injured, want to invest time alone instead of with the accomplice, feel defenseless when engaging in sexual relations, and feel that they need to ceaselessly recover their own vitality when it gets cluttered with that of their accomplice. They might be so terrified of getting to be overwhelmed by someone else that they close up genuinely just to endure.

- The sick, the afflicted, and those with frail limits are attracted to the unrestricted comprehension, and empathy of an empath emanates without monitoring it. Until you figure out how to close out the vitality of others, you may have a really hopeless reality wherein you have a feeling that you must be altogether alone so as to endure.

It's anything but difficult to perceive any reason why being an empath is frequently extremely depleting. It is no big surprise that after some time, a few people shut down their empathic capacity. What's more, with that, they likewise shut down an imperative piece of their celestial direction framework. Figure out how to deal with the measure of data vitality you get and hear a greater amount of what is extremely significant.

15 empath gifts

Empath present form #1. Physical intuition

With this type of empath boon, sometimes you understand what's happening in another individual's body.

Empath gift form #2. Physical oneness

With this type of empath boon, the way you get information is near home. On your body, you feel somebody else's physical procedure to be at this instant.

Empath gift form #3. Scholarly empath ability

With this type of empath boon, you proceed into another individual's scholarly wavelength.

Empath gift sort #4. Passionate intuition

With this kind of empath boon, you understand what's happening in somebody else's feelings, no matter whether another person is hiding a part of that. E.g., joe behaves lively yet feels stressed.

Empath gift sort #5. Enthusiastic oneness

With this next type of empath boon, you similarly find knowledge about the fact with respect to what's new with somebody else's opinions. Only the data shows up distinctively compared to psychological intuition.

Empath present form #6. Otherworldly intuition

With this type of empath blessing, you've got the advantage of falling the way the individual partners with god.

Empath gift form #7. Otherworldly oneness

With this type of empath boon, you've got a direct experience of how a person interfaces together with the divine.

Empath gift form #8. Creature empath

With this type of empath boon, you understand what it looks to be a particular creature.

There are monster darlings. And then you will find monster darlings who have been similarly having ability and experience as monster empaths. A substantial immense contrast...

Empath present form #9. Organic empath

With this type of empath boon, you have the uniqueness of different scenes. To you, it is not the only view.

Empath present form #10. Plant empath

With this type of empath blessing, you understand what it looks to be a particular blossom or herb or shrub.

As a talented empath, you are going to find this capacity so beneficial for nurturing, maintenance of crops, cooking!

What is more, as you're talented (competent, however talented as an empath), prepare to get your mind blown. You won't cover the expense of lasting alongside tasting the pieces of knowledge.

Empath present form #11. Precious stone empath

With this type of empath boon, you go in the cognizance of a gemstone or semi-valuable rock.

As a gifted empath, you'll have some great times with assorted stones. Really, even small gems and precious stones may prove to be revolutionary wellsprings of information, inspiration, otherworldly investigation.

Empath present form #12. Mechanical empath

With this kind of empath boon, you encounter what looks to be a system. You feel what it requires. You may have the choice to resolve a machine, irrespective of whether you do not have technical learning how to fix that type of equipment. Haha. As a talented empath, you'll have the choice to receive your money's worth -- and then some -- out of some other machines that you utilize. Additionally, what an outstanding bit of leeway you've got for adapting new improvements, applications, etc!

Empath present form #13. Fixing empath ability

With this type of empath boon, it's possible to learn things, without being told, regarding points of interest with another individual's wellbeing.

Empath present form #14. Empath talent with astral beings

With this type of empath boon, you can have immediate comprehension of some kinds of astral animals, confirming whether they are blossom pixies or celestial attendants.

It is vital to understand that empath talent with astral beings does not mean that you"must" turned into a channeler or moderate.

Empath present form #15. Atomic empath ability

With this type of empath boon, even one of the empaths, you're ultra-insightful about folks. It would be perfect if you notice, this can be a very uncommon blessing. In reality, it is more than being enthusiastic or discerning or curious.

Appreciation to your boon, chip away in your qualities, and enhance

6 Tactics to turn being an empath into your best gift

1. See time as lonely

In our existing reality where there's by all reports, therefore, a great deal of stress, dramatization, and pessimism, it's crucial for touchy individuals to have time to think and also to process feelings. Without time to focus on separate needs, empaths may feel overpowered by the demands of others.

Make seeing time as lonely a necessity and use a chance to achieve the things which help you with staying sound and adjusted. You could realize that contemplation, shamanic venturing, representation, drifting in character, journaling, or painting can help you with handling feelings and concerns.

2. Discover a room to revive your energies

It can earn a space in which to rekindle. You require a place that's quiet and calm and at which you will not be distracted by external impacts. For certain people, building a contemplation area, either at the home or nursery, can help.

For other folks, investing day daily energy in character reestablishes them. You may also shield yourself at the washroom for a few tranquil times daily if that's the major spot you'll find some stability.

Cause your area is as beautiful as possible with candles, the function of plants or anything else puts you in a quiet view. Try to make sure your space is not cluttered or cluttered, as an unmistakable space can still help the mind.

You may additionally prefer to use basic or incense oils to boost your area, and a couple of people like to use quieting songs or contemplation software to allow them to reestablish.

3. Shield yourself from negative energies

Being an empath, touchy into the essentials and feelings of others, maybe sincerely depleting. Try to protect yourself from a lot of negative impacts where possible. Utmost time went with contrary, harmful or basic individuals and found time to reestablish when you are with them. Steer clear from damaging media and focus on news that is inspirational and stories that are positive.

4. Discharge negative energies

Regardless of the sum, you guarantee yourself, you may once in a while get negative opinions out of everyone about you. You may likewise find yourself stuck in unhelpful believing layouts about your personal. Empaths are in no way, shape, or form lively and constructive always, and distress to the planet and many others may frequently bring touchy people into discouragement as well as trouble.

All these feelings should not really be seen as unwanted. Anguish and problem are ordinary in a faulty world, and denying that these thoughts will not make them vanish. Instead, try to feel that the feelings entirely and then have them pass. You are able to use apparatuses, for instance, journaling, moving, or exercise, to assist procedure cynicism.

5. Use your empathy to benefit the entire world

Empaths instinctually understand the planet's difficulties will not be handled by abhorring and dismissal however by adoration and understanding. Try to use this energy positively for the earth, irrespective of whether it's only in small actions, as an instance, committing to some nutrition bank or obtaining clutter.

Having the choice to achieve something useful to the entire world owing to your compassionate character is going to aid you with being sure about being an empath instead of considering it as a burden.

6. Pursue your own dreams

Since empaths are so delicate to the requirements and feelings of others, they could once in a while ignore their own fantasies. However, remember, you're a novel otherworldly being who's in this world at the moment using a motivation supporting your own. Attempt not to allow other people to burn the majority of your energy to the stage you don't have anything left to present your personal dreams.

Types of Empaths

Compassion is simply the endowment of having the option to place yourself from another person's point of view and feel things as though you were them. Be that as it may, there are a few distinct kinds of empaths, every one of which has an alternate arrangement of compassionate capacities.

The 6 fundamental sorts of empaths are:

1. Enthusiastic Empath

The enthusiastic empath is one of the most widely recognized sorts of empaths. If you are this sort, you will effortlessly get the feelings of others around you and feel the impacts of those feelings as though they were yours. The enthusiastic empath will profoundly encounter the sentiments of others in their very own passionate body. For instance, a passionate empath can turn out to be profoundly pitiful around another person who is encountering bitterness.

For passionate empaths, it is critical to figure out how to separate between your own feelings and those of others. Along these lines, you can utilize your capacity to help other people without getting to be depleted.

2. Physical/Medical Empath

Those with this sort of sympathy can get on the vitality of other individuals' bodies. They naturally recognize what distresses someone else. Numerous individuals with this sort of compassion become healers either in the ordinary restorative callings or in elective ones. Physical empaths may 'feel' mindfulness in their physical body when treating somebody. They may likewise 'see' blockages in an individual's vitality field that they sense need treating.

If you are a medicinal empath, you may get on manifestations from others and feel them in your own body. Assuming the physical side effects of others may prompt medical issues. A few people with interminable sicknesses, for example, fibromyalgia or immune system illnesses, may discover it fortifies their very own vigorous field so they can kill this capacity when essential. Taking some preparation in a type of mending can likewise sharpen this capacity.

3. Geomantic Empath

Geomantic sympathy is here and there called place or natural compassion. Those with this capacity have a fine attunement to the physical scene. If you get yourself awkward or extremely upbeat in specific conditions or circumstances for no evident explanation, you might be a geomantic empath.

If you are a geomantic empath, you will feel a profound association with specific spots. You might be attracted to consecrated stones, forests, houses of worship, or different spots of sacrosanct power. You may likewise be delicate to the historical backdrop of a spot and have the option to get on bitterness, dread, or delight that have happened in areas. Spot empaths are exceptionally sensitive to the regular world and lament for any harm to it. They watch with loathsomeness when trees are chopped down, or scenes are devastated.

If you are this sort of empath, you will presumably need to invest energy in nature to revive. You may likewise discover helping in a natural task recuperating for you. It is likewise significant for you to cause your ordinary surroundings as agreeable and delightful as you can. You may feel more joyful if you fill your home with plants and characteristic fragrances. You may likewise prefer to pick common materials, for example, wood and cloth, for your garments and furniture.

4. Plant Empath

If you are a plant empath, you instinctively sense what plants need. You will be green-fingered and have a genuine present for putting the correct plant in the opportune spot in your nursery or home. Many plant empaths work in parks, nurseries, or wild scenes where they can put their blessings to great use. Indeed, if you have picked an occupation that includes plants, at that point, you are presumably a plant empath. A few people with this blessing really get direction from trees or plants straightforwardly by hearing it inside the brain.

If you are this sort of empath, you will definitely realize that you need a ton of contact with trees and plants. You may get a kick out of the chance to fortify this bond by sitting unobtrusively by an uncommon tree or plant and adjusting all the more near its needs and direction.

5. Creature Empath

Numerous empaths have a solid association with creatures. Be that as it may, a creature empath will likely dedicate their lives to working for the consideration of our creature companions. Those with this blessing will comprehend what a creature needs and might have the option to clairvoyantly speak with the animal.

If you are a creature empath, you likely, as of now, invest as a lot of energy with creatures as you can. You may find that considering the science or brain science of creatures causes you to refine your blessing. You could likewise consider preparing as a creature healer as your uncommon ability can empower you to discover what's going on with a creature and treat it as needs be.

6. Claircognizant/Intuitive Empath

If you are a claircognizant or natural empath, you will get data from other individuals essentially by being around them. One look at somebody can give all of you sorts of knowledge into that individual. You will quickly know whether somebody is misleading you since you can detect the goals behind their words.

Those with this blessing reverberate to other's enthusiastic fields and read the vitality of others effectively. This is firmly identified with the clairvoyant empath who can peruse someone else's musings.

If you have this capacity, you have to encircle yourself with individuals with who you feel lined up. With this blessing, you may need to fortify your vivacious field, so you are not continually barraged with the contemplations and feelings of others.

Being an empath isn't simple. You may think that it is confounding, disorientating, and debilitating. Be that as it may, understanding which of the sorts of empath you are can assist you with using your blessings and capacities to support yourself and everyone around you.

Conclusion

If empaths have been incessantly exhausted by injury or stress, they may require a prescription for discouragement and nervousness to adjust their organic chemistry. I suggest recommending these principally for the present moment. Strangely, I've seen that numerous empaths require a much lower portion than other individuals to get a constructive outcome. For example, a fragment of a stimulant can do some amazing things for exceptionally touchy patients. A standard doctor may discount this as a "fake treatment reaction." I oppose this idea. How drug influences empaths and touchy individuals are more exceptional than you may suspect. Empaths are simply progressively touchy to everything, including meds. We frequently can't endure the typical dosages that regular drug regards viable.

Continuously ask yourself, "What is my body's reaction to prescription?" It doesn't make a difference in case you're the one in particular who at any point had a symptom, if you experience something, it IS genuine. I get so tired of specialists letting me know, "Well, you're the just one to encounter _____, so it must not be genuine!" As an empath, I've figured out how to confide in my body, most importantly. I trust you do as well.

What's more, I'm likewise entranced by new research about how torment drugs can repress compassion. Ohio State University scientists as of late found that when members who took Tylenol (Acetaminophen) found out about the incidents of others, they appeared less terrifying than the individuals who didn't get the medication. Along these lines, if you have a contention with a relative and you had quite recently taken Tylenol, this exploration proposes that you may be less sympathetic. Realizing that Tylenol diminishes sympathy is significant since 52 million Americans take a substance containing it consistently!

It is essential to know how medicine influences empaths and delicate individuals. In case you're an empath who needs medicine, I recommend working with an integrative human services expert who comprehends unobtrusive vitality so you can locate the best measurement for your body. Make certain to impart to your PCP how your body reacts to the portion of the prescription you are given so you can control it if important. Most significant, make some noise if you are awkward. Keep in mind, the purpose of taking any drug or partaking in any restorative intercession is to concentrate on your recuperating.

Numerous things can meddle with psychic capacities, including the accompanying:

Psychic Myths

One case of a psychic fantasy is in case you're psychic, you should know it all. Truly, even the best psychics just realize what they should know. Such confusions can make you question your psychic capacity, in this way, diminish your capacity.

Your condition

It's normal to be incredulous of psychic capacity since the vast majority experience childhood in a situation that doesn't empower it. Be that as it may, unreasonable demoralization or, more terrible, deride by loved ones puts a genuine damper on your common capacities.

Mishandling your capacities

Prying into others' lives and endeavoring to control individuals isn't your right, and abusing your psychic ability will bring about negative karma and square your otherworldly movement.

Intuitive feelings of trepidation

These can be from the present life or previous existences. For instance, if you were executed by strict experts in a previous existence for setting out to restrict the Church or straightforwardly applying your otherworldly capacities, you'll normally feel dread about these subjects. Previous existence relapse can enable you to reveal and discharge the negative feelings.

Medication use, liquor misuse, and a few prescriptions

Indeed "simply pot" can hinder your instinct and misshape your world. When you be as clear of a channel for the Light as could reasonably be expected, it's simpler to satisfy your potential and benefit as much as possible from your time on Earth.

Stress and outrage

Outrageous feelings and stress can hinder profound direction from the opposite side.

Neglecting to have some good times

Setting aside an effort to play will make you feel glad and loose, an ideal state in which to get psychic knowledge.

Your own planning

It's entirely expected to experience cycles in which your psychic capacity appears to be lessened. These can keep going for a considerable length of time, weeks, months, or more, and be distinguished through thorough crystal gazing and numerology.

The vitality of other individuals

We find that we are increasingly psychic with individuals who have a more prominent than normal psychic capacity and can feel hindered around cynics or individuals who are obstructed in different manners.

Lost spirits and dim elements

This is a major one, more typical than a great many people acknowledge and frequently misjudged. It's imperative to clear your vitality intermittently. Consuming sage can help, yet for progressively obstinate vitality, attempt our Spiritual Detox sound and, or the book Spiritual Clearings by Diana Burney. Her book will enable you to demand help from various more elevated level profound assistants on the opposite side to clear otherworldly trash you may have gotten incidentally (which is anything but difficult to do).

Diet

Nourishment bigotries, medical issues, synthetic compounds in nourishment and anything you put on your body, an excessive amount of caffeine, a lot of low-quality nourishment, an excess of sugar (even organic product sugar), and more can make you feel blocked. The more delicate you are, and the more psychic you are, the more these things can meddle.

Take a stab at utilizing reflection day by day for unwinding. After a timeframe, when you feel progressively focused, request help from your aides of the Light, at that point, center on straightforward inquiries to recover your certainty. Having confidence that you will realize what you have to know, when you have to know it, will conquer any hindrance to supportive knowledge. In time, and with training, you ought to feel increasingly psychic.

Printed in Great Britain
by Amazon

85836841R00054